CLAIMING KIN

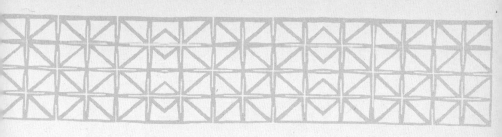

CLAIMING KIN

Confronting the History

of an

African American Family

AFI-ODELIA E. SCRUGGS

ST. MARTIN'S PRESS ≋ NEW YORK

History • Travel

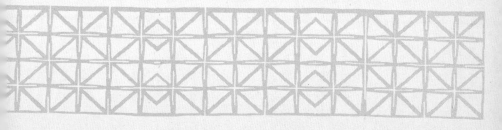

www.stmartins.com

Library of Congress Cataloging-in-Publication Data

Scruggs, Afi.
　　Claiming kin : confronting the history of an African American family / Afi-Odelia E. Scruggs.—1st ed.
　　　　p.　cm.
　　ISBN 0-312-26135-7
　　1. Scruggs, Afi.　2. African American women—Biography. 3. Scruggs, Afi—Family.　4. Scruggs family.　5. African American families—Tennessee—Nashville.　6. African American families—Tennessee—Williamson County.　7. African Americans—Biography.　8. Nashville (Tenn.)—Biography. 9. Williamson County (Tenn.)—Biography. I. Title.

E185.97 .S38　2002
976.8'5600496073'0092—dc21
[B]

　　　　　　　　　　　　　　　　　　　　　　2001048739

First Edition: February 2002

10　9　8　7　6　5　4　3　2　1

This book is dedicated to my ancestors,
who taught me all that it means to be
a Scruggs.

ACKNOWLEDGMENTS

Back in 1994 I sat down with my pencils and a legal pad to draft the outline of a book I hoped to finish within a year. The book was to be a how-to manual on performing gospel music. The writing was to be creative but straightforward, demanding little from the reader and, most importantly, the author.

But the ancestors had other ideas. My book on gospel music turned into an oral history on traditional hymns, and then a book of personal essays about sacred songs that had played a large part in my life. I was writing one of the chapters when the ancestors finally spoke. The result is the book you now hold.

Yes, writing this book was a journey. One does not travel alone and I have many people to thank for helping reach my goal.

My agent, Janell Walden Agyeman, has been a rock. Her faith in my abilities has never wavered, yet she does not hesitate to steer me in the right direction. She believed in this book when word counts, deadlines and my own expectations hindered the flow of ideas. I thank you from the bottom of my heart, and hope our relationship lasts many more years.

I'm also indebted to Glenda Howard and Monique Patterson, editors who saw the potential in this manuscript, and helped me shape it.

I must also thank Thelma Battle of Franklin, Tennessee. Her interest in the history of blacks in Williamson County started as a hobby and grew into an obsession. She was there whenever I dialed her number—mostly in the wee hours of the morning—and didn't mind talking for hours. She is a treasure and I'm sure the ancestors sent me to her.

I'm grateful to Louise Lynch, who directs the Williamson County Archives, Doris Douglas, who heads the county's genealogical library, and Rick Warwick, author of *Williamson County in Black and White*. They are rich sources of knowledge and I learned so much from talking to all of them.

I wrote much of this book while working as a reporter in Cleveland, Ohio. Many of my colleagues had my back in a big way. Their questions, and occasional teasing, kept me on track and close to deadline.

Finally, I have to mention my family: my mother and siblings, my nieces and nephews, my aunt and cousins, and especially my husband, Jubal. Their pride in my efforts touched my heart. I hope I've lived up to their expectations.

Prologue

This is how I remember my father.

He is wearing a white suit. His pants are rigidly creased, testifying to twenty years in the Navy. The suit is brilliant against his dark brown, almost black, skin. His hair is mixed gray, as are his beard and mustache. They are the only hints to his age, around forty-nine or fifty. He has no wrinkles. His face is as firm as it was when he was in his thirties.

We are in church: Pilgrim Emmanuel Baptist Church. It's the church my father grew up in and away from. When he returned, out of nostalgia, perhaps, or an impending sense of his mortality, he came without his wife and children. Our home church was my mother's church across town. My father wasn't lonely at Pilgrim. He had family there: his sister and her two daughters.

My sister and I are visiting this particular Sunday. Maybe there was a special service, a baptism or Women's Day service. Maybe we just impulsively decided to go to church with Daddy that morning. He was so happy to have us there with him, he spontaneously arranged for me to sing a solo. I rolled my eyes and leafed through the hymnal. I sang "Even Me."

Now I'm seeing my father a little later, after the sermon has ended. We all stand, my sister, my aunt and cousins, indeed the entire congregation at the preacher's command. My father is in front. My sister and I are in the pew directly behind him. He turns to face up, stretching his hand across the wooden bench. He shakes my hand and then my sister's. He is leaning slightly, to greet the folks beside us. The church is singing.

This may be the last time, this may be the last time children,
This may be the last time, may be the last time, I don't know.

The song signaled the close of service. Pilgrim's members didn't sing until after the doors of the church had been opened to receive the repentant. The sinners would walk up the aisle, each step taking them farther from the pleasures of the world. They would sit in front of the entire congregation, their simple presence an admission of their transgressions.

A deacon would move that the sinner be allowed to join the church "with all rights and privileges of a member in good standing." "You've heard the question," another deacon would announce to the congregation. "Are you ready to vote?" The congregation would answer "Yes," always yes, always ready to bring the outsider into the fold, into the loving embrace of the heavenly Father. Then it was time to sing, to remind the young and mature children of God that salvation depended on the will of a seemingly capricious master.

Perhaps it was because of such rituals that I'd always associated "May Be the Last Time" with slavery. Maybe it was the tune, which is identical to "Wade in the Water." Perhaps it was the refrain, the constant repetition of the phrase "I don't know." I do know the song felt like folks who were intimate with powerlessness, who understood how chance and circumstance could alter one's life, had composed it.

But the song doesn't carry me back to slavery as it once did.

Whenever I hear it now, in the years since Daddy died, I'm trans-
ported to Pilgrim Emanuel. I am standing in front facing my
father. I am reaching for his hand.

I am clasping air.

My father, Max Walter Scruggs, Sr. died too soon. He was
only in his early fifties, just at the cusp of his life. He'd come
up hard, in a family so poor that he'd begun working at five
years old. When he died, he had finally acquired the trappings
of success: a nice house; a Cadillac and a Lincoln parked in the
carport; children in good colleges; an impressive wardrobe.

My father was an accountant. Such work wouldn't count for
much now, since blacks are routinely corralled into middle man-
agement. In the 1970s, however, we were just rising up out of
manual labor. A teacher was considered a professional. Black
Nashvillians were accustomed to professors and doctors—the
city is home to two black universities and one black medical
school—but those people were the social and professional elite.
The masses cleaned houses, euphemistically called "day work,"
or held the other laborious positions reserved for society's low-
est.

My daddy had become an accountant after a career in the
Navy. The GI Bill sent him to Tennessee State University, the
public institution created for black folks. He had donned his
cap and gown just a week after I'd worn mine to my high school
graduation. My status as the oldest child made me the first of
my siblings to graduate from high school. Daddy, the youngest
in his family, beat circumstances to graduate from high school
and college.

After graduation, he worked as a comptroller for Fisk University, one of the "Ebony League" schools. From there, he became an auditor for the State of Tennessee. Later, he took a job
with a federal program that helped blacks set up small busi-

nesses. When he died, he was managing money for a black entrepreneur.

Daddy had "good" jobs, the kind of work that other blacks mentioned with a tinge of envy. They wore uniforms: blue jumpsuits or light blue shirts and black pants. My father wore suits. They pushed brooms. My father pushed pencils. They lifted boxes, but my father lined up figures. His work was quite an achievement for that time.

Still, it wasn't enough for him. I never knew him to sit back and relax, to turn his head over his shoulder and gaze down the road of his life. I never knew him to exhale and smile in mild amazement over his journey from nobody to somebody. But then, I never really knew my father.

Perhaps that's why "May Be the Last Time" evokes the scene at Pilgrim Emmanuel. Chance and circumstance snatched my father so quickly, I wasn't able to prepare for his departure.

"Come home," my mother said. "Your father is sick." She'd called me on a sweltering afternoon, tracking me down at my boyfriend's apartment. Summer in Rhode Island, where I was attending graduate school, was nothing compared to Tennessee. Still, August is August wherever you go. Down South, we had air conditioners. In New England, we endured the heat wave with glasses of iced coffee and lots of cold showers.

"What's wrong?" I was irritated that she'd called, but frightened by the afternoon's interruption. Mama was known to be dramatic. Now, though, her voice was subdued. I sensed that she didn't want to tell me.

"Come home," she repeated. "You've got to get home."

"But I don't have any money!" My parents had been skeptical of my academic aspirations, especially my decision to study

Slavic linguistics. Black folks went to graduate school, true, but nobody wasted time studying *that*. I could do whatever I wanted, but I had to pay for it. And I did, depending on fellowships and summer jobs. My budget was rigid and relentless. There was barely enough space for rent, much less an airplane ticket home.

"Come home." She hadn't even heard me. There was no mention of a ticket, no suggestion of a loan.

"Tell me what's wrong," I insisted. "I don't have the money."

I was getting angrier and more annoyed. I'd left home, escaping to college at sixteen to avoid these kinds of demands, and I had become adept at keeping my family at an emotional distance. I talked to them, especially Mama, several times a week. But I could and did go for years without a visit. I belonged to them, but my place was at the edges. I entered their circle cautiously, unwilling to submit to their expectations.

"You have to tell me. I don't want to worry all the way to Nashville, if I can come."

"Your father has lung cancer."

When I got home, Daddy had finished surgery. When I left, he was at home. But he was fading. He'd never been a large man; Mama and I argued over whether he was 5'9" or 5'11". But after his discharge from the hospital, he wasted away so much his house robe seemed to swallow him. His limbs were lifeless sticks, brittle as the branches of a dying tree. His voice was as inconsequential as an afterthought; breathing took all his strength and concentration. When I got back to Rhode Island, I called home more than ever, making a point to speak to him. But he answered in single syllables and passed the telephone to my mother.

Still, I wasn't prepared in November when a campus security guard found me at a gospel concert. "You have a telephone call from home. . . ." the officer said softly. By the last word, I'd grabbed my coat and pushed past the person sitting beside me. I ran out of the auditorium, my best friend behind, searching for the closest private telephone.

"You need to come home," my sister told me when I called her. "Daddy is in a coma. I'm going to be honest. He died once, but the doctors brought him back."

"Why are you telling me now," I complained, my fear sounding like annoyance. "Why did you wait?"

"We didn't want you to worry," she said. "And don't cry. We love you."

My best friend held my hand the entire time. Somehow, others had followed or found us: a preacher from a local church, the students who sang in the choir with me. Just five or six people, but enough to fill the room. My friend asked the preacher to pray. "Our heavenly father . . ." he began. With my mouth to God's ear, I whispered words of my own. "Please don't let my father die. Please let Daddy live." When I got home, I packed a dark blue skirt, a somber blouse, and a pair of black pumps.

Daddy's death elevated minor comments into monumental pronouncements. Insignificant meetings became important because they were all I had. Times we shared, and thought we'd share again, became final events. The church service was one of the last times I stood with my father.

I think. I question this scene, even as I put it on paper.

Why had I come to church that day? Was I home from school on semester break? That doesn't seem right. If I didn't have the money to come home when Daddy was hospitalized, a trip home between semesters would have been an extravagance. But I dropped out of grad school for a year, just long enough to catch my breath and decide whether I wanted a career delving into the minutiae of immigrants' English. Maybe I'd gone to Nashville to wait for my boyfriend and drive to California. We'd decided to spend the year in Los Angeles. He'd work on his dissertation and I'd decide what I wanted to do with my life.

If this part is right, then I was home around September 1979. That doesn't feel correct either, because Daddy was wearing a white suit. Nashville's fall is almost indistinguishable from its summer, but my father wouldn't have worn a white suit after Labor Day.

I don't think. At least I don't think he would have. I just don't know.

I'm sure we shared a laugh, my sister and I, when a young girl walked up the aisle to join church. She was a "fox"—that's what they called gorgeous, sensual women then. Her legs were long and her dress was short, just barely over her behind. And the dress was red enough to light up the town on a Saturday night. You just didn't wear something like that to church unless you'd been in the world a long, long time.

But what had Daddy said that made us press our lips together and battle to keep quiet? I can't remember. And I can't fill in the gap because I didn't know my father well enough to insert his words into the blank. His death left me without his voice, his words, without the story of his life.

Our family's stories came from my mother. She unwound the past so expertly, she could have been descended from the West African jaliyaa. Like those oral historians from Mali and Gambia, she revealed the lives of people who died years before we were born. Mama led us along streets in neighborhoods long demol-

ished, taking us into houses that had collapsed from abandon-
ment and neglect. Her tales were complete with plots and
subplots, conflicts that resolved halfway or not at all. We kids
thumbed through her life like it was a novel, returning time and
again to our favorite parts.

"Tell us about Willetta."

Willetta was our cousin, a wife and a mother when we were
gazing at pre-adolescence. She was a distant relative, really. Our
maternal grandparents had been brother and sister, so she, like
us, belonged to the third generation of my mother's family. We
only saw Willetta once every two or three years, if that often.
Her branch of the family lived in New York; the rest of us lived
in Chicago or Tennessee. They were Jehovah's Witnesses, while
we were Catholic or Baptist. We had other cousins her age, but
we didn't ask to hear about them as much. Willetta was special.
She was "something else."

That description was the ritual phrase, which opened the
story, the obligatory beginning of a ceremony guaranteed to end
in laughter.

"Tell us about Willetta," my siblings and I demanded.

"She was something else," my mother responded. She
shook her head over the recollections of her younger cousin.
"Willetta was bad." Mama accented the last word to make us
understand that Willetta acted worse than we ever imagined.

"What did she do?"

"Willetta had a crush on Max. When he came to visit me,
he'd wear his dress white uniform. We'd sit on the front porch
in the glider . . ."

"The same glider that's out there now?" The glider on my
grandmother's porch was a relic from the fifties. Its metal hinges
had survived years of humidity and summer thunderstorms, but
the weather had its effect. The glider squealed whenever it

rocked. The squeak convinced us that the glider was ancient enough to have decorated the porch during our parents' courtship.

"No, not that glider," Mama said, playing her part in prolonging the story. "Another one. And Willetta would bend over, rub her hands in the dirt and then rub them all over your father's uniform."

As young as we were, and I, the oldest, was around eleven, we understood the depths of Willetta's affront. In the "service," rules were rules. Creases had to be sharp enough to carve a diamond. Whites had to be so bright, angels could have worn them to work. Such audacious naughtiness was as thrilling as watching Larry and Moe poke Curly in the eye. It was unbelievably dangerous, so provocative, so bad!

"What did Daddy do?"

"He jumped up, screaming and yelling. I just laughed," Mama said.

"What happened to Willetta?"

"Nothing, I think."

Now we knew Willetta ruled the house. She had trespassed on my father's precious time with his girlfriend, sentenced him to hours of washing, starching, and ironing—but nothing happened to her. If we'd done something like that, our behinds would have been introduced to a switch—and the entire community would have received detailed reports. We would have never heard the end of our transgression, not even after we had kids or grandkids.

But Willetta got away clean, without a whipping or even a lecture. She'd disrupted the house for a second, then everything returned to normal, just like Curly did after Larry and Moe's assaults. Such a reprieve was extraordinary. We ran to get Daddy's side of the story.

"Tell us about Willetta," we demanded.

"Willetta was a pest," he answered. He wouldn't look at us for watching television. His feet were up on the table and his hands were behind his neck.

"Did she mess up your uniforms?" we pressed further. But Daddy didn't break.

"What did your Mama say?"

"She said Willetta used to rub her hands in the dirt and then rub them on your dress whites . . ."

"Then that's what happened."

We left and went somewhere else, probably to annoy Mama so she'd order us to go outside and play. Daddy was comfortable in his solitude. He wasn't letting anyone in.

The years since my father's death have given me little insight into the reasons for his silence. Was he merely a quiet man, as stingy with his words as he could be with his money? Or was his aloofness a hedge that concealed and protected him from outsiders? All I have, so many years after his death, are the facts of his demeanor. My father was a taciturn man, who lived in a society that revered the art of small talk. "Speak ass, 'cause mouth ain't got no sense," my mother once commanded, when my father—again—walked through a room without greeting her guests. She succeeded in embarrassing him, so he would, from then on, acknowledge her friends. But his greetings were soft and inaudible, as if the words were reluctant to leave his mouth.

Sometimes there were surprising openings in his hedge. When I was in my mid-twenties, really just a couple of years before Daddy's death, I brought Jim, my white boyfriend, home. Just having him in the house was enough to get the whole neigh-

borhood talking. We were, after all, in a Southern city still burying memories of sit-ins, boycotts, and busing to achieve school
integration.

Jim and my father, however, formed an immediate bond. I
saw them sitting, talking together, and realized I'd fallen in love
with a young, white version of my father. Jim's wanderlust
wasn't as compelling as my father's. Daddy had sailed all over
the world, while Jim had only driven across the country two or
three times. But their curiosity had taken them to out-of-the-way
places.

They sat in the den for hours. Daddy stretched out on the
turquoise vinyl couch (Jim hated that couch; he thought the
color, accented with glitter no less, was unbelievably gauche),
while Jim searched for a comfortable position in the matching
red vinyl armchair. They roamed orally, comparing experiences
in California, then New Mexico. "Your Dad really liked California," Jim told me later. "He said he'd wanted to stay in Santa
Barbara, but your Mom wouldn't hear of it. She had to be close
to her mother." I shook my head, imagining Daddy's expression:
his eyes locked steadily on Jim's face, never shifting downward
or sideways. Daddy's voice would have been even and dispas-
sionate, hiding any lingering feelings over my mother's intran-
sigence.

Jim had taken me to Santa Barbara. We had stopped there
to relax after driving along the Pacific Coast Highway on our
way from San Francisco to Los Angeles. To me, travel was a
means to an end. I preferred the shortest route from the place
of departure to the destination without meandering along the
way. Jim was so infatuated with the journey that the destination
was almost an afterthought. For every trip, he pored over tour
guides and sent away for brochures. The trip became a foray

into regional history and culture, sometimes an excursion into the past, depending on the sites and sights his research uncovered.

The stop in Santa Barbara had no larger significance. It was just an opportunity to escape Jim's '65 Mustang, to stretch our legs and inhale fresh air. We ate in a city park, I think, covering the picnic table with napkins in place of a tablecloth. The wind whipped up the paper, so we ended up eating with our elbows on the table, bending our faces down to eat our sandwiches.

When we walked along the beach, I looked over my shoulder and giggled like a child at the footprints I'd left. The waves of the Pacific Ocean rolled so softly to the shore, I couldn't help but remember the angry, breaking waters of the Atlantic, a continent away. In Russian, the Pacific is called the "Quiet Ocean." The words sounded like the waves rushing to the shore. I savored that phrase as I drew a deep breath and worked to memorize the scent of the salt and the serenity of the moment.

I'd seen the Pacific when we stayed in San Francisco. But the experience was still new to me, a Tennessean accustomed to grassy hills that slowly but surely swelled into limestone mountains. Tennessee had beautiful lush landscapes, alternately curvaceous and angular. There was, though, no sea stretching beyond sight, rolling and shifting according to the moods of the moon.

My father had spent his adult life at sea. He'd learned the sailor's skill of shifting his weight according to its rhythms. I knew I would miss the sea because I wasn't sure when I'd see it again. My father missed it because he had lived on top of and under the waves.

I felt a kinship with Daddy deeper than our relationship as parent and child. I knew why I was standing in the sand, listening to the waves and storing their whispers in my memory. My father's genes were drawing me to the sea.

I'd felt my father on that beach, and again while listening to Jim. So it didn't matter that a virtual stranger to my family had been allowed past defenses I struggled to penetrate. It didn't matter that my father had revealed himself to a man he'd known only a few days, but not to me.

I don't mean to imply that my father was a man without voice or words for his family. He was not one to disappear by dissolving into his surroundings until he was indistinguishable from the walls and furniture. His presence spoke when he did not. We always knew when Daddy was around, even if we weren't sure where he was.

My father had a way of stealing up on us, usually when we were doing things we had no business doing. Like talking and giggling instead of falling asleep.

The room my sister and I shared was across from my brother's. Instead of going to bed and closing our eyes, we went to bed and opened our mouths. We teased each other, aiming our taunts through the open doors, sure they'd fly straight to the target.

"Go to bed."

That voice, way too deep for a child, silenced us immediately.

"Didn't I tell you to go to bed?"

Somehow, Daddy had crept up the stairs and eased down the hallway. His silhouette surprised and threatened us into obedience. We piped down and immediately fell asleep.

Now that I'm an adult, although not a parent, I've developed a few tricks of my own for dealing with children. I realize now that Daddy didn't slip down the foyer. We were talking so loudly, we couldn't hear the stairs creak when he came upstairs. What we took for anger was probably exasperation over having to get out of bed and tell us to keep it down.

Maybe. Daddy did have a way of sliding around the activity in our house, slipping out the den door and driving some-where—anywhere—else. I think the rest of the family was so preoccupied with each other, the chores, with the radios and folks dropping in, that Daddy probably just got up and walked out of the door. We simply didn't notice his absence until he was long gone.

The way to reach Daddy was the way Jim had done it: to sit down with my father in his element; to talk softly, casually allowing the conversation to flow as it would. My father wasn't one for the jokes and quips that decorated my family's conver-sations. He wanted to savor his talks, like he sipped the glass of scotch and water he kept on the coffee table.

When I sat down with him, really settled into place and slowed the pace of my words, I found the gaps in his hedge. Then we had talked: about his tour of duty in Vietnam; about fighting to defend a country that, because he was black, denied him the right to vote for his commander-in-chief; about joining the Navy to prove he was smart enough to pass the entrance test. And sometimes my father would open up enough to talk about his brother William.

My father never laughed over his brother's idiosyncrasies or pulled out a story about some prank William had played. Did my father even know these kinds of things about his brother? I don't think so. Daddy was seven years younger than William, too young to grasp the details of William's personality, maybe even too young to see him as anything other than the big brother.

Still, I know my father adored him. Daddy never said it. I could hear it when Daddy called William's name. The way my father's voice lingered over the syllables turned a first name into an invocation. And, as the story unfolded—it was always the same story—Daddy stopped saying William at all. He called his brother Bubba.

When that happened, the story was close to its end. I listened intently, hoping that something new, some other emotion would color Daddy's voice. I wished for resignation or acceptance. I always heard pain, sorrow, and guilt.

My father was the last person in the family who saw William alive. William was only fifteen when he died, just months after his father's death. Those months, though, turned William into the man of the house and an authority unto himself. His father had managed to keep him under control, but his mother—my grandmother Dora—couldn't handle her oldest son. When she ordered him to stay home, William simply climbed out the window.

" 'Don't tell,' " my father said. "He made me promise not to tell. And you know, he was my big brother, so I just grinned and kept quiet."

If my father hadn't kept that promise, what would have happened? Maybe Bubba wouldn't have died?

Bubba was shot by a white storeowner who had been robbed, and he'd warned William and the others not to come back.

"When the white man saw Bubba, he said, 'I shot the wrong one,' " my father told me, recalling details he had been told. Nothing happened. In the 1930s, a black boy's life didn't count for much, especially if he'd been warned, especially if the shooter was white. My family buried William and my father buried his memories, as if keeping his promise not to tell. Some memories, however, live as strong as weeds, rooted deep within our consciousness and surviving every attempt to kill them.

The mourners sat shoulder-to-shoulder, forcing latecomers to stand against the walls of the church. I don't remember what the preacher said, how he tried to comfort us, to convince us that my father's spirit had long abandoned the corpse lying in the casket. But I do remember the soloist, Diane, singing "We Are Our Heavenly Father's Children." The pianist had added jazz chords to this traditional gospel hymn, and the unexpected progressions took me out of my grief. For a minute.

As I listened to the notes, absorbing the new character of the familiar song, I heard other sounds: Diane's voice, confidently reminding us that "God knows . . . just how much we can bear." I heard the exhortations to "Sing, girl!" that encouraged her to pour her heart into the words she was directing at us. And I heard crying; not polite sniffles, but sobs and moans. I turned around to face my cousins.

Daddy had two nieces and eight nephews. Almost everyone had made it to the funeral. I looked at his nieces. Were they the ones I'd heard? But they sat upright, their eyes on the pulpit as if to deny the tears flowing down their cheeks. The sobs came from their brothers, broad-shouldered men with sons and daughters of their own. When we were little, those cousins had clamored to come to our house. Their visits lasted for days, turning our quintet of parents and children into a pair of adults riding herd over ever so many kids.

My father's name alternated between "Daddy" and "Uncle Max." He laid down the law when required, and abandoned the whole crew when the noise and activity overwhelmed him. Had he been around to see my cousins clutching their children, comforting little ones bewildered by their fathers' moans, Daddy would have snapped, "Be quiet. Men don't cry."

They were crying, not because they were weak, but because they'd lost the man they had looked up to. They acknowledged their sorrow, and the proof of their love ran down their faces, falling onto the children squirming in their arms.

As I looked at my cousins, my tears met theirs. I'd been self-absorbed, grieving the father who now lived only in my memories. Now I cried for my cousins, who'd lost their uncle. I grieved for my Aunt Helen, who was burying her last sibling.

I cried for my mother, who was missing Daddy's key in the door. And for my brother. He'd learned to be a man so well that he couldn't weep at his father's funeral. I cried for my sister. And I cried for myself.

I missed my father. I wanted him sitting in the pew next to me. I wanted to walk into the den and see him sleeping on the turquoise vinyl sofa. I wanted to hear his snores compete with the static from the television. I wanted to laugh when he jumped up to mutter, "I was watching that," after I'd cut the TV off. I wanted to see him anywhere but there, laying in a coffin, his hands resting on the lapels of his navy blue suit.

After my father's funeral, I counted up my memories and found them painfully meager. I remembered Daddy in pieces, like vignettes from a larger play. I kept replaying the scenes, hoping what I had would nudge me into recalling more. But I couldn't get past the little I already had. So I decided to do for my father what he hadn't been able to do for me. I decided to recover the stories and relationships that would reveal his place among the generations of his family.

Our past would finally have shape and weight. It would sit on a shelf and never again be lost.

Descendants of Dick Scruggs

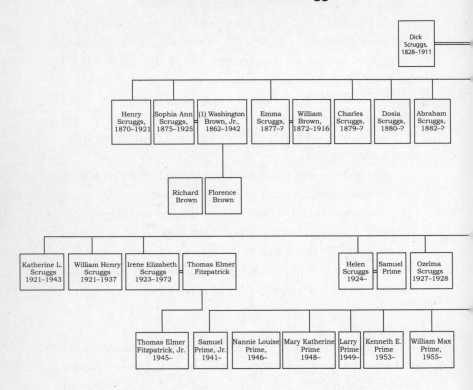

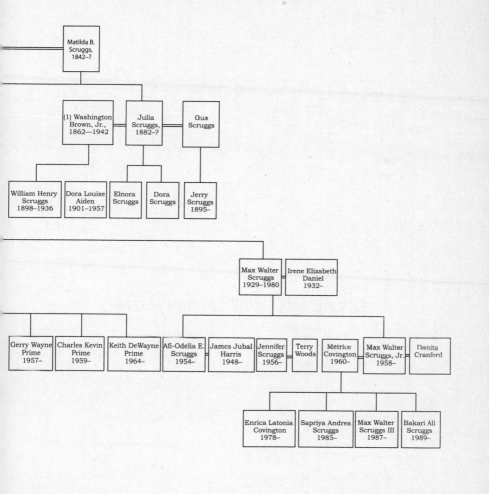

Descendants of Max Walter Scruggs

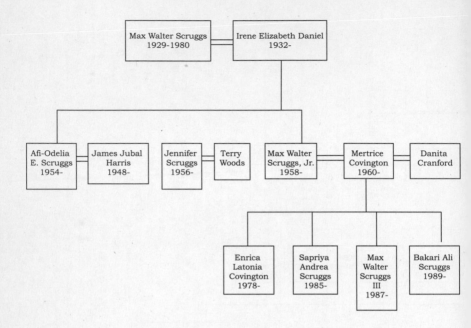

Descendants of William Henry Scruggs

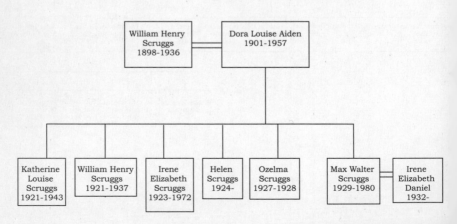

Descendants of Julia Scruggs

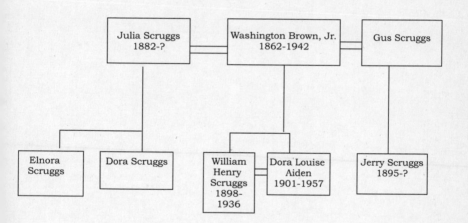

PART ONE

Chapter One

I'd always heard we had the wrong last name. Instead of Scruggses, we should have been Browns.

The comment was never whispered like an unwilling confession. It was simply stated as an accepted fact. We lived in Nashville, but we came from Franklin, Tennessee. And we should have been Browns.

"Why?" I asked my Aunt Helen. "How did the Browns get into it?"

I pulled out my notebook. I'd approached my task the same way I'd prepared for my college papers. I wanted names, dates, addresses, facts. Stories and rumors were okay, but I was after information that would lead me to documents and records. I would collect that paper and arrange it chronologically. I would capture everything I'd learned between the covers of my notebook.

"I don't know," she answered. But I didn't believe her. I prodded her, confident that the right question would lead me to a lode of family lore.

"What about your grandmother, your father's mother? What was her name?"

"Julia, Julia Scruggs."

"She married a Scruggs, right?"

"Yeah. His name was Washington."

"Well, what was her maiden name? Was she a Brown?"

"I don't know." Aunt Helen stretched out the last two words. Her voice rose, as if she were questioning what she thought she knew, holding it up against her recollections of old conversations. "All I know is Scruggs," she said, her voice falling in a final apology.

"Do you have any pictures?" This was a desperate request. Aunt Helen lived in the projects. The accumulation of her lifetime had been pared down to fit into the few rooms given to single adults without children. If she had snapshots, I was sure they would be filed in drawers or buried under boxes in her closets, where they wouldn't take up much room. But she reached over to the end table jammed between the wall and the couch. She rummaged under the Sunday comics and pulled out a statue.

It was small, not quite six inches tall, but thick and heavy. When she handed it to me, I saw it was a bottle encased in concrete. Someone had tried to make it pretty; bits of seashells protruded from the cement. The bottle contained a tiny picture. I held it up to my face and saw my grandmother and grandfather, Dora and William Scruggs. I brought the bottle closer and squinted, trying to make out their features. But I could barely see their faces.

I set the bottle down carefully in the spot she'd made for it. "Do you remember anything else?" I asked. "Anyone else?"

She knew of two aunts, her father's aunts really: Emma and Dosia. "Daddy lived with Aunt Dosia when he moved to Nashville. Aunt Emma married a Brown."

"Folks always said we should have been Browns instead of Scruggses."

My notebook lay open, but the pages remained empty. I could remember the little I'd learned: aunts named Emma and Dosia; great-grandparents Washington and Julia Scruggs; and a surname that clung to our family, although no one knew why.

> *"(There is no shame) in going back to fetch it."*
> —the Asante proverb, Sankofa

A noted art historian, Maude Wahlman, once told me why so little from Africa survived the Middle Passage. In Africa, the elders guarded knowledge, releasing it only after the student was initiated into the mysteries of wisdom. The young people understood everything learned carried some kind of responsibility to the society. True erudition, the proverbial mix of wisdom and understanding, came only with age.

Slavery, however, depended on bodies vigorous enough to survive weeks of starvation and confinement. Slave traders wanted the young, whose will to live would prevail against despair, filth, and their own fervent prayers for death.

"So much was lost," she told me. "So much was lost."

It took me several years to plumb the depths of her explanation. We had been discussing Congolese symbols, crosses encased in circles believed to open the road to the spirit world. I was chasing spirits, but I'd overlooked the path stretching in front of me.

I thought I was recovering history when I collected details. When I tugged a story out of my aunt, I brandished it, convinced that I'd rescued another bit of my family's past from oblivion. People, places, and dates were the links in the chain

I was forging to reconnect the generations, and I valued only the new, ignoring what I already had.

I didn't consider my aunt's life because I thought I knew it all. Helen Scruggs Prime was the fourth of six children. She had nine of her own, with just as many grandchildren and a few great-grandchildren. She lived in the projects in south Nashville, the same side of town where she'd been born.

I excelled in interpretation and analysis of data. But no elder had taught me how to hear meaning in things unsaid, or to search for the evidence of things unseen. I recorded my aunt's ignorance in the same desultory way I'd summarized her life. I'd accepted the fact that my aunt didn't seem to remember much about her family. I didn't ask why.

When I matured enough to recognize my errors, I invoked Sankofa. I retraced my steps and returned to talk to Aunt Helen.

"What do you want?" My aunt's delaying tactics had failed. Dinner hadn't distracted me: I filled up on family gossip with every forkful of macaroni and cheese. She'd washed the dishes and rearranged the refrigerator to hold the leftovers from the evening meal. She'd swept the floor and wiped off the stove. She'd drained the sink and laid the dishrags on the counter to dry. And finally, she'd settled into her chair.

"What do you want?" She sighed, puzzled over my insistence that she lay out her life for my notes. I didn't know how to make her understand: how frightened I was of losing my last few recollections of my father; how much I needed stories to shore them up.

"Anything," I begged, "a story, something that happened when you all were little."

"Ahh," she started, exhaling her reluctance and resignation, inhaling the strength to look back. "Life was so hard for us."

She spoke briefly of standing in relief lines, of walking home in bitterly cold weather without a coat because they didn't have anything else to hold the food they'd gotten.

"Bubba used to shovel coal at Vanderbilt. He got fifty cents a week. When he got paid, we'd get to go to the show. . . . It was warm. . . ."

There were four of them: Katherine, Bubba, aunts Irene and Helen. The tickets took most of Bubba's money.

". . . He had a dime left over, and he used to buy a sweet roll. We'd split it four ways. . . ."

"What about Daddy?"

"What . . . ?" Aunt Helen squinted, dazzled by the light reflecting from the cinder block walls of her apartment. Pictures, in frames and albums, competed for space in the étagère. Her family stood in those pictures behind her: her oldest son in his Air Force uniform, a younger child in his; two grandchildren standing on their mother's lap at a photographer's command. I had pulled her away from her siblings, giggling and talking in the dark movie theater. I'd brought her back to a small apartment on a busy street corner, and a life where she, because she was the survivor, had become the matriarch by default.

"What about Daddy?" I repeated.

"Your daddy wasn't born yet," she said. "He made five."

As I drove home, I repeated her words until I could see the people in them. The images were imperfect. After Aunt Irene's death, when I was in college, I'd come across a picture of Katherine. The photograph was thirty years old, a good decade older than me, and the woman smiling in her good coat could have been my mother. We shared a straight nose with thin nostrils, a white folks' nose that contradicted our full lips. I had her brown eyes, she had my naturally arched eyebrows. But that was Katherine as an adult, not as a child. I knew as I drew my mental portrait that I was actually drawing myself as a sixth-grader, giving my aunt French braids and a big bow instead of the ponytails and plastic baubles my friends and I had worn in our hair.

My aunts Helen and Irene were younger versions of themselves, with the fully formed limbs and build of an adult. I worked to make them younger still, shrinking their arms and legs, raising their voices to imitate the fourth-graders I'd heard. They must have been kids, I figured, maybe nine or ten. Bubba and Katherine were a bit older, probably in their teens.

"Bubba used to shovel coal at Vanderbilt. He got fifty cents a week. . . ." I framed my pictures, using facts to crop out extraneous details. My grandmother Dodo saw 1921 come and go with two babies in her arms. Katherine had been born on New Year's Day; Bubba arrived just two days before Christmas. Aunt Irene was next, in July 1923. Another year, 1924, meant another baby: this time Aunt Helen in November. Ozelma was born in September 1927 and died April 1928. My father was the last one to come, in March 1929.

"Your father wasn't born yet. . . . He made five."

Suddenly, sadly, I was looking at children. Not youngsters who lived in a world with dinner with the family and cookies after school; not kids who enjoyed baseball with Daddy and whined about baths before bedtime. My elders were shivering, hungry children. Aunt Helen's favorite pillow was a leather armrest. She and her siblings, snuggling under the warmth and darkness, dozed to the dialogue from the movie screen. They rested, contentedly licking sweet, sticky fingers until the lights came up, the ushers roused the audience, and everyone had to go home.

When I got home, I presented all this to my mother, the

way I'd done when I'd busted my knee as a four-year-old. I needed now what I needed then; someone who understood, who would say the right thing without prompting.

"It hurt me so bad, when Aunt Helen told me," I said to Mama. "To know . . ."

". . . they were cold and hungry, and so little. . . ." she answered. Maybe she could see what I was trying to visualize: a boy, no older than eight, working like a man to feed his sisters; children filling their stomachs with pastry and purchased shelter.

"Your father always felt inferior because he couldn't provide for his sister. . . ." Mama added. That surprised me. Aunt Helen was married, and if Uncle Sam didn't care about his wife and children, why should Daddy feel guilty?

I, however, was thinking like a child and not like a sister. As young as I was—in my twenties, then, and still feeling my way through life—I desired the best for my sister and brother. I wanted to see them happy, in a good home and comfortable enough to risk some adventures with their money. I wanted all this for my siblings, and we were children of privilege, certain that clothes would always hang in our closets, that we'd own at least one pair of shoes. My father and his siblings hadn't climbed a crystal stair. They'd stumbled over bare places, spots with no rug on the floor.

I looked in our living room, noticing, for the first time in years, the carpet cushioning the entire first floor. This was my father's dream for his sister: a soft place to walk, some solace for her feet when the going got hard.

". . . He hated it when she moved into the projects," Mama said.

"But he had helped her!"

Daddy had taken his sister to apply for a place, steering her to a friend who'd worked in the housing authority office. Maybe he saw this as the final comedown. I remember Aunt Helen living in houses that were larger, and originally more opulent than ours. Eight of her nine children were home, so she rented old mansions with bay windows and turrets and an attic big enough to house another family. But that side of south Nashville was fraying around the edges, and the houses showed it. The porcelain fixtures were chipped, the hardwood floors were scarred, and the yard was unkempt. But the tree in back was big enough for two kids to lounge in its branches, while the third one of us clambered up the trunk. The neighborhoods were safe enough for us to run up and down the block without a backward glance toward the house. And the rents were low. So Aunt Helen stayed, moving within a two-block circle, until the city decided to make real money on the properties. Whole neighborhoods were demolished for Music City USA recording studios, and record companies took over the lots where my cousins and I roamed. The people who'd lived there were out in the cold.

Aunt Helen teetered on the edge of homelessness until her husband finally found a place across town. The oldest children were grown and gone. She and five youngest ones were crammed into a two-room shack, relying on an ancient coal stove for heat. There was no place to play. The yard was a plot of fatigued dirt that might have nurtured grass once upon a time. Inside, smoke and hopelessness polluted the air. When she moved back to south Nashville and into the Edgehill Projects, even I was perceptive enough to be relieved.

"... Helen told him 'Max, I'm doing the best I can ... ,'" Mama said.

And she was, whatever my father thought. With nine children and an off-again, on-again husband, she'd worked and

kept everyone together with a roof over their heads. She'd cared for them, fed them, gotten all the kids through high school and into the world. She did for them, as the old folks used to say. Whatever it took, she'd done it, and done it better, perhaps, than her mother had done for her.

"Where was their mother?" I asked. This was the way Mama and I talked, picking up threads of topics we'd dropped and weaving them into the conversation at hand.

"She was weak." Mama spoke with the even confidence of someone whose eyes provided the evidence for her judgment. "She would cook food and let other people eat while her own children went hungry."

"Where was their father?" Mama turned to me, expecting some insight into spaces between the lines of Aunt Helen's story. "He hadn't died. . . ."

"No," I interrupted. "This was before Daddy was born, re-member? I don't know where their father was."

Aunt Helen hadn't said and I wasn't going to ask. I couldn't, really. In the name of Sankofa, I'd picked up this discarded memory and found myself struggling under its weight. I'd turned around to retrieve a part of the past, and I wasn't eager to go farther.

But I had to. I was only a few steps into this journey, and was still a long, long way from the crossroads.

Chapter Two

*"They say the black Scruggses descended
from a white man named Ned. . . ."*

My mother and I sat at the kitchen table, talking and fidgeting in the chairs. Mama had browsed through a lot of showrooms before finding these chairs. They were black, and the wrought iron backs looked like the grill on our security door.

She'd bought the chairs for the table we'd had since forever. I'd practiced my alphabet on it as a first-grader. But the chairs were "new," even though they'd been in our house a good fifteen years.

She had searched carefully for those chairs. They had to complement and modernize a Formica holdover from the 1950s. For we had finally bought our house. Like a bride on her wedding day, Mama had something old—that was the table. She needed something as new and strong as the hope she carried across the threshold with the suitcases and furniture.

Mama understood this would be her only house. Even as late as 1967, when my parents took on the duty of writing a monthly mortgage check for the next thirty years, you lived in your house until you died. She'd yearned for a "fabulous" house, filling the adjective with all the expectations of magic and surprise that spurred her search for the unique, and often gaudy.

"You know what I want?" she'd say, pausing long enough for us to realize she was asking, not telling. Then, before a word left our lips, she'd answer. "I want a circular house, every room a round room, so I'll never have to vacuum corners.

"You know what I want?" She would chant it, just like we sang "Miss Mary Mack" in circles with friends on the playground. "I want a house with seven bedrooms, so I'll only have to make the beds on Saturday."

If wishes were horses, beggars would ride. My father was in the Navy and my mother taught school. They surrendered to their finances and bought a white colonial.

You couldn't miss it. Turquoise columns flanked the front door. The shutters on either side of the windows looked like the blue eye shadow we piled on our eyelids when we dressed for parties. Visitors walked into the foyer with their heads tilted, blinking at the miniature lights twinkling in the filigreed brass chandelier. They stopped at the top of the stairs to stare at the orange and green tweed sofa, nonchalantly resting in its wood veneer platform. If they were brave—or they knew my mother very well—they lounged in the green easy chair in front of the picture window, lit up a cigarette, and flicked the ashes into the hanging ashtray.

If they knew Mama well enough to have seen one of her tantrums, they shook their heads and headed into the kitchen. Then they perched on the vinyl seats of the chairs and sipped a cup of coffee.

You had to be careful, because the chairs were as treacherous as they were gorgeous. If you forgot yourself and relaxed against the high backs, the chairs would tip from the weight of your body. Lots of us, friends and family, ended up sprawled on the floor. Plus, the chairs had spindly legs that dug deep into the linoleum. When we walked into the kitchen barefoot, our toes sunk into the dents.

"We're going to keep this place nice," Mama vowed and threatened when we'd put the boxes into our rooms. "We'll do it," we kids promised—and we meant it. We would wash dishes and put everything away as soon as we finished eating. We would hang up our clothes. We would only sit on the couch when company came. We would play in the den.

We stayed on our guard for about a year. Then we wore socks in the kitchen and slid on the floor like ice skaters. The dishes piled up. The counters stayed cluttered because we couldn't find anywhere else for the can opener and coffeemaker and the other stuff that appeared so mysteriously.

The wear on our house and our nonchalance about it confirmed our change in attitude. The white colonial with the loud, blue trim was no longer a showplace attesting to our ascension into the middle class. It had become our home, the center from which we radiated. We had drawn closer, even if we were not together.

Daddy's death, in 1980, had done that for us. It had shown us life is as short as a breath and any breath might be the last.

My brother, Max junior, came home, moving his first wife into the old room upstairs. They left after a few months. Then he returned alone; without a father, without a wife, balancing grief and anger across his shoulders like a tribal woman toting water.

A teaching job took my sister, Jennifer, to Chattanooga. It wasn't far, two-and-a-half hours away. But the highway heads out of the rolling hills surrounding Nashville and into the limestone peaks of the Appalachians. Jennifer's accent marked her as a foreigner. She, on the other hand, struggled to understand her students. "I don't try to motivate them to go to college," she told me once. "This is east Tennessee. It's good if I can get them to finish high school."

I'd even taken a few steps toward the family circle. I'd taken my new doctorate to Virginia, first to teach at the university in Charlottesville, later to work on my writing in Richmond. Getting to Nashville took some doing: two hours from the eastern coast into the Blue Ridge Mountains, then another five to Knoxville. It took three more hours of driving, watching mountains diminish into hills, before I could park the car in Mama's driveway. But I was no longer living on the edge. I was connected to the region and the family. When I talked, no one stared and asked "Where are you from?" No one wondered when my family emigrated from the Caribbean islands because "your name sounds so strange. . . ." I was not quite home, but I could get there. And, for the first time in years, I wanted to.

I can't say exactly when my mother and I sat in the kitchen, teasing each other about the shaky chairs that hadn't broken—yet.

"Watch that chair," I told her. " 'Cause I ain't picking you up off the floor." Then I reached back to turn the radio down. It seemed that radio had been on since we moved into the house. The music had changed, from Motown and Stax to funky bands and disco, but the station had remained the same for years.

I absentmindedly traced the designs on the tabletop with my finger, trying to follow the squiggly black and gray lines covering the Formica.

It felt like 1969, when my father had retired from the service. We kids spent the weekend standing in the sliding glass door downstairs, listening for his car. When the black and yellow Camaro turned onto the patio, we started jumping up and down. "Daddy's home," we shouted. "Daddy's here!" Mama, however, stood her ground in the kitchen. She'd given him two days to get home before she filed for a divorce. She was broke, and school wouldn't start for another month. Her silence tempered our noisy joy, but it couldn't destroy it. We clung to his legs, and wrapped ourselves around his body while he climbed the stairs to face her anger. Her first words were about money. Did he have any? No, he didn't. A few days later, they sat at the table juggling figures, trying to pay bills and fill the refrigerator.

But my father was dead. He'd been dead long enough so that our sorrow had diminished from barbed agony into a manageable throb. We could talk about him now, dredging up good and bad times with no fear of disrespecting his memory. So it was sometime in the 1980s. I cannot tell you when. When doesn't matter anyway. The what and the why are more important.

I was sitting at the same kitchen table my parents bought before I started school, trying to relax in chairs my mother bought to decorate the grand new kitchen in her grand new house. I was thumbing through the past, searching for a why to add to the what and who of my identity. I was questioning my mother, preparing to claim a history that I wasn't sure belonged to me.

From my vantage point as a child of the civil rights era, segregation is an inextricable puzzle. I'm not talking about the mere separation of the races. Segregation was more complex than blacks on one side and whites on the other. The rules of the system were as irrational as the system itself: separate bathrooms and water fountains, but black cooks in white homes; separate schools, but black women raising white infants. Yet those who lived in that time understood where the boundaries lay, what lines could be crossed by whom and how.

To me, who came of age watching "white only" and "colored only" signs disappear from stores and restaurants, it is a wonder that a white man could have sat in my grandmother's house and chatted with the family. It is a wonder that my maternal relatives—my mother, grandmother, and great-grandmother—could have welcomed him into their home, surprised that he'd taken time to come by. It is a wonder that blacks and whites could have been cordial, or that a white man might have knocked on the door because he was in the neighborhood and wanted to see how things were going.

I know, however, that it happened. That's how my mother learned about the Scruggses.

A white man, an insurance agent from Franklin, told my mother about Ned Scruggs. The agent had known my mother's family for years. At first, their relationship was built on business. He came by the house in west Nashville, my mother's childhood home, for the fifty cents premium that promised a decent burial for my great-grandmother. When my grandmother and her sisters pooled their money and bought their mother a nicer brick house, across town in north Nashville, another agent took over. The weekly ritual, however, continued. The new agent would knock on the door, about the same time on the same day. They'd all make small talk while my great-grandmother pulled the small, manila envelope out of the drawer. She'd give the agent the money, he'd mark the payment in her book and his. Then more conversation as he walked out the door.

Southerners love such rituals, elaborate despite the outward simplicity. Like segregation, they're unfathomable to those who didn't or don't live with them. Why not have the money and papers on the table, pay the insurance man, and go back to whatever it was you were doing before he came? I think, though, our Scotch-Irish and African ancestors must have demanded we maintain the graceful tradition of putting people before commerce, of acknowledging a relationship before getting down to business. And I think the roles played out every week, the courtesies extended and accepted, somehow tied people together. So impossible as it seems to me, a child of the liberated South, a white insurance man could have sincerely missed his old customers.

Maybe he turned onto Arthur Avenue and thought about my great-grandmother and grandmother. Perhaps they'd been prompt, always ready with a payment, among the best customers he'd had. As he drove down the street, he caught sight of the brick house with its modest gray porch, and he wondered, how are those folks doing?

So he pulled up to the curb and parked his car. He walked up the steps, noting my great-grandmother's flowers lining the railing, just like he was used to. Then he rang the bell.

And he might have gotten a smile when my folks answered the door, a smile and, knowing my grandmother, a loud "Hey, how're y'all doing?!" They were surprised and happy to see him.

They invited him into the house and offered him "a little something": a slice of cake, a glass of iced, sweetened tea if it was hot, or a cup of coffee if the mild chill Southerners call winter had descended over town. If he was hungry, he refused twice before accepting. If he wasn't, he refused twice, explaining that he'd already eaten in order to apologize for turning down their hospitality. Then my grandmother and great-grandmother sat down across from him. "How y'all been?" he'd say. And the rite began.

"How's your son in Chicago?" "What about your oldest brother, the one that lives in New York?" The conversation resembled a call and response: his questions, their answers, his comments and theirs. Sometime during this exchange, my mother stuck her head in the room. Yes, she told him, she had finished Tennessee A&I. She wasn't teaching, though. She'd been in New York. She'd gotten married. She wasn't a Daniel anymore, but a Scruggs.

"Hey," the insurance man said. "You've married a descendant of Mr. Ned Scruggs!"

They say Ned Scruggs had a wife, Mrs. Nellie. But he wouldn't stay with her. He stayed with a black woman. . . .

Ned Scruggs's story was quickly told. He'd had a wife, a real wife, who folks called "Miz Nellie." But his heart belonged to a black woman named 'Ariah. She had his children.

"Folks said Mr. Ned would fight you over those . . . children," the insurance man said. But Mama always stuttered at that point in the story. She said the man meant to say "nigger children," until he remembered his hosts and his manners.

That was our family history, reduced to a couple of sentences recited in less than five minutes. What remained unsaid was worth hours of contemplation.

Mr. Ned Scruggs had a wife in name only. He openly lived with a black woman. He loved their children enough to fight for them, and those fights, together with his commitment to 'Ariah, turned Mr. Ned into a legend.

Mr. Ned belonged to every story I'd ever heard about Southern race relations. His situation was best discussed in whispers and speculations about white folks with "black blood." We recited it as proof that we were better, more distinctive than the ordinary, garden variety Negroes who lived next door and down the street.

It was too common and too easy. Although I'd kept quiet, I had questions.

Just who was Mr. Ned? Which of his children lay at the roots of our family tree? My suspicions showed in the tilt of my head, the way my lips slid into a tight line.

My mother remained nonplussed. She was used to my doubts, and probably expected me to check out the story for myself. She knew that I, of all her children, believed in written words over spoken ones. I would want my information to be verified and visible, not mythologized and audible. She waited while I looked for a way to express my reservations without rejecting her story.

"Did Daddy ever talk about this?" After all, he was the one who was born a Scruggs, not Mama. He should have at least heard of Mr. Ned and Mrs. Nellie, of a black woman who was the mother of half-white children.

"He didn't know," Mama said. "I told him."

The white man told my mother. She passed the story on to my father. With each retelling, the skeletal facts gained flesh, finally standing firm as the truth of our family's origins.

It didn't matter to my father that he'd never heard of this white man, Ned. My mother knew the insurance agent, had been acquainted with him for years. That was all Daddy needed.

Again I stood on the outside, trying to understand what I'd observed and heard. I was raised to be a person of the book, but my parents and their fore-parents were people of the word. They judged those words by the teller, by all they knew of his or her life. It didn't matter if the details changed, if the teller fashioned the story to his or her liking, as long as the essential truth remained embedded in the center.

My father had seen his love fully reflected in my mother's eyes. They had taken vows to support and cherish each other, vows that were as potent and vibrant as they'd been the day they had been made. My father believed this story because my mother told him. And she would not lie.

Chapter Three

My mother was sitting at a table when she heard about Ned Scruggs. This was the table where all of us, she, her husband and children, pulled up chairs at Thanksgiving and Christmas. It was the table she left in anger at a family dinner, when my grandmother chided her for putting too much food on her plate.

This table still sits in the middle of my grandmother's dining room. Its legs are huge, gripping the floor like the roots of an ancient oak. This table is as much a part of my family as the Formica dinner table in Mama's kitchen. She stood at the head of that old Duncan Phyfe table on her wedding day, sliced her cake, and took her first taste of life as a Scruggs.

My mother claims she was "meant" to marry Daddy. She personally sealed their fate at thirteen, when she meticulously and repeatedly wrote "Mr. and Mrs. Max W. Scruggs" in the margins of her notebooks and papers. This is one of Mama's more recent stories. She started telling it after Daddy died and she became infatuated with a Pentecostal-style, Spiritualist church.

Pentecostal people, the ones mainstream black worshippers

call "Holiness," believe that you can ensure a blessing by "claiming" it. If you are right with God, fervent and disciplined in your prayer life, if you study the Bible religiously to show "thyself approved," like Paul's apprentice, Timothy, you can simply grab what you want—in Jesus' name, of course. What you are really doing, through prayer and worship, is aligning your will with God's. Therefore, God will honor your claim. You are asking for what you deserve.

At thirteen, Mama spent Sundays sitting next to her grandmother in one of Nashville's oldest black Baptist churches. My great-grandmother appreciated Holiness people. They could, at least, dance if possessed by the Spirit of God. Baptists believed you could dance yourself right into Hell. My great-grandmother had been quite a dancer in her youth. She didn't, however, fool around with claiming blessings, and she didn't teach it to my mother. Mama said she practiced the law unconsciously, as directed by Spirit.

"Yeah, right," I said, whenever she trotted out the story. "You just had a crush on Daddy."

She laughed, but she didn't deny it.

Mama liked the ugly, skinny boy she met in summer school. Those are her words, "ugly" and "skinny." "We were all ugly back then," she told me, trying to sweeten her description so that I'd find it more palatable. "We just thought we were cute."

I'm sure, though, she was being honest. She and her friends probably did think Daddy was ugly. When my parents were young, good looks equaled light skin and straight hair. Daddy's skin was dark, a deep warm brown that hinted at black. His hair was kinky, so tightly rolled that each strand had to be brushed and greased into submission. Blacks wouldn't appreciate those attributes for another three decades, when we grew our hair, clenched our fists and proclaimed "Black is beautiful!"

Plus Daddy was bony and probably graceless. At seventeen, when adolescents begin to make peace with their bodies, he was still all arms and legs. A snapshot from his first year as a Navy seaman shows a man-child, standing at attention with his arms by his side while his hands dangle aimlessly. His head looks huge, a dark blob without eyes or nose; the brilliant white seaman's cap eclipses his features.

Mama said the Navy was good for Daddy, that starches and meat three times each day put weight on him. He even grew a few inches. So at fifteen, when he was still at home with his mother and sisters, Daddy must have looked like a stepchild in a fairy tale: malnourished and so destitute that getting through each day was a battle and a victory.

Daddy was ugly, shy, and just mysterious enough to pique Mama's curiosity. "You know, I'll talk to anybody," she said. "But I'd say something to him and he'd just look at me. And I'd say to myself, 'What's wrong with this fool?' "

School was the only thing my parents had in common. Nashville had its "Black Bottom," true. But the city had no single area so distasteful—and worthless—that whites decided it was only good enough for "niggers." Nashville's blacks lived in distinct neighborhoods on three sides of town: north, south, and west. Whites had east Nashville all to themselves. They had lynched a man once and hung his body from a bridge. Not long after, a fire destroyed that side of town. The calamity was God's punishment, black folks said, but fire didn't burn away the memory of a body swaying from a noose. Blacks stayed away, from that side of town.

They lived in ghettos. Not slums, where houses slump on their foundations while flowers struggle to camouflage broken glass and cracked curbs, but neighborhoods resembling Warsaw and Lodz before barbed wire and Nazi guards. Custom and laws kept Nashville's blacks in their place, but what was meant to separate turned into a refuge.

My mother lived in west Nashville, while Daddy lived in south Nashville. Getting to Daddy's side of town took an hour by bus, with at least one transfer. She stayed in the neighborhood, for school and college, until her marriage took her to New York. Daddy's family stayed put, too. They lived in a lot of different places, but they didn't move away from their side of town.

My parents' lives ran on parallel tracks of the black, Southern experience. Mama stood before her congregation and gave her life to the Lord, while Daddy rose from the baptismal pool in his church, swaddled in white and free from sin. Mama walked to Washington Junior High School, while Daddy went to Cameron. Their lives converged in the same place where generations of black Nashvillians met: Pearl High School.

If you were black and went past grammar school, then you passed through the halls of Pearl High School. You had no other choice. Pearl was the city's sole black high school, and therefore the institution that linked disparate sections into a single community. When you couldn't identify a person by church or neighborhood, one question placed him among friends and relatives: "When did he finish Pearl?"

My parents belonged to the class of 1948. Their class portrait documents their presence at the school, as it illustrates their relationship. The students' pictures were arranged alphabetically. Mama, a "Daniel," came early in the "D's." Daddy was on the line with the "S's." My parents moved in the same sphere, though not necessarily in the same circles. Surrounded by their friends, sitting in different rows in the same classrooms, they eyed each other from a distance. Pearl didn't make them close friends, but it introduced them. That was enough.

Two years later, my father ran into my mother at Nashville's black public park. He'd joined the Navy and come home on leave. She was in college, studying to become a teacher. They talked and exchanged telephone numbers. He proposed, for the first time, three days later.

My grandmother is a stickler for accuracy, which she defines as *her* version of events. When I mentioned my parents' wedding and the legend of Ned Scruggs, she hurried to set me straight.

"Your mother was married in the living room," Elizabeth said. She emphasized the final two words, as if reminding me that she was there, that my parents hadn't even conceived of me yet.

"I know that," I said, adding some emphasis of my own. Mama and Daddy got married in the living room in front of the fireplace on May 19, 1952. Their wedding pictures have hung on my walls for years.

My father is looking down at my mother. He is not a tall man, maybe 5'9" at most. But Mama is barely 5 feet in high heels. Her outfit emphasizes her petite stature and her feminine shape. The ankle straps on her shoes show off her small feet; her wedding dress caresses her waist like my father probably did on their first night together. Mama faces the camera with a smile bright enough to substitute for the flash. She confronts the instrument, challenging its capacity to record her happiness.

But Daddy only has eyes for his wife. His face is in profile and the camera captures his smile. He stares at her, absorbing each detail: the white cloche perched on her black curls; the small corsage she holds instead of her bouquet; the pleats falling from her waist and grazing her hips. My father embraces my mother, supporting her with his right hand. He stands close to her, so the pants of his suit brush against her wedding dress. He inclines his head toward her and smiles, amazed and joyous that this woman has agreed to share his life.

Had I ever seen my father gaze at my mother the way he did in those pictures? I recall a relationship as fragile as a porcelain bowl, which somehow withstood the fissures threatening its existence.

My parents fought: over money; my father's poker games; my mother's stubbornness. I don't rely on astrology for guidance, but my parents' signs captured their temperament. My father was an Aries, my mother a Capricorn. Ram and goat locked horns repeatedly, turning tiny disagreements into major power struggles. Each argument chipped away at the marriage, marring the perfection my parents envisioned when they stood in my grandmother's living room.

Still, the marriage never shattered, despite the cracks winding through their relationship. I look at the wedding pictures and I see a love that survived almost three decades, as if nourished by the years of fussing and fighting.

I see the devotion that would keep my mother sitting in intensive care for days, counting the waning hours of her husband's life. I see the pride that would inflate her voice when, twenty years after Daddy's death, she bragged about her twenty-eight years with her first husband.

The wedding pictures predicted my parents' love would last through death, and it did. My father was and is a constant presence in my mother's life. His spirit roamed the house, making its presence known to my stepfather, Johnny. He saw my father when my mother couldn't and told her, "Max is standing there," in the bedroom, on the stairs, sitting in the kitchen.

My parents had a true love, if not a perfect one. Ram and

goat, they lowered their heads, butting each other until their contests exhausted them. When they finally realized compromise was not a synonym for surrender, it was almost too late.

Daddy would be dead within a couple of years.

Weekends were hell at our house. My father came home late, if at all.

I think after staying out past midnight Friday, he figured he should give Mama a real reason to raise sand. So he remained wherever he was, doing whatever he did until Sunday evening. He had to come home then, to sleep off his hangover and get himself together for work the next day.

We kids spent the weekend in fear of Mama's temper. Her anger at Daddy accumulated and churned until it turned into a raging cloud. We were caught up in the inevitable whirlwind. There was no place to hide.

We just had to endure.

Sometimes enduring meant sitting on the couch in the living room, waiting for the storm to break over our heads and drench us in shouts and commands. The dishes were never washed quickly enough, the kitchen was never cleaned thoroughly enough. We wanted to leave, but were scared to ask for permission to visit our friends; a simple request might bring a lecture about staying out in the streets instead of being at home.

We knew she wasn't talking to us, but to our father.

I'm still not sure what all Daddy did from Friday to Sunday. The first of the month was payday, and that weekend he gambled. He counted poker hands, while Mama, at home, counted up the bills. He always came home broke.

Other times, he drank and hung out with his friends until late. Then he went to a lady's house. If he told me her name,

I've forgotten. But he assured me that she wasn't a girl friend or a mistress, just a refuge.

"I just go there to sleep," he said, "when I don't want to be bothered with your Mama's mouth."

I sympathized. I often wished I didn't have to be bothered with my Mama's mouth either. But I never blamed him for the sarcasm and short temper she displayed when he wasn't around. He could have been at home all day and the atmosphere would have still been tense. My mother wanted a husband who took her places, who played with the children, who worked in the yard—even though we didn't really have a yard.

Daddy just wasn't that kind of a parent. He was the kind of father who would send his children to school without lunch money, confident that they would find a way to eat. Depending on Daddy was like standing on shifting sand.

Mama was our rock.

She didn't eat, so we could. She browbeat Daddy into giving her money for Christmas, then she used it to buy gifts for us. We loved Daddy, but we needed Mama.

She tried to leave us once, and I tried to stop her.

She'd gathered us in the den, maybe in her bedroom. We were somewhere downstairs, not in the living room or the dining room where she usually broke important news. That's why her announcement surprised us so.

"I'm leaving," she said. She watched us carefully, waiting for Jennifer to cry, or maybe Max, or maybe even me. She was going to a friend's house, she said, and gave us the address and telephone number.

"Don't tell your Daddy where I am," she said. "If he asks, tell him you don't know."

She wanted us to lie for her, and I was willing to do it. I

loved my father, but Mama had found and bought this house. The house Daddy found—his way of showing her who was boss—was tiny and even more poorly constructed than this one. She came up with the mortgage money. She made sure the light and the heat stayed on, and food was in the refrigerator.

I was about fifteen and dreaming of college. It would be my escape from shouting and hostile silences. But that evening, I pulled my sister and brother into the bedroom for a quick conference. Then I went back to Mama.

"We want to go with you."

She looked surprised, as if she had not expected such a quick, decisive allegiance. Her eyes softened. She missed us already. But her bags were packed and her car key was in her hand. She would spend that night and the next worrying about us, straining to keep from picking up the telephone to check on her children.

"No, you stay here." She left to go and ran into my father. She spoke before he could. "I'm leaving."

"Where? Why?"

She didn't answer either question. I knew the answers to both, but I didn't open my mouth. Telling where she would be, why she was leaving, would mean inserting myself into adult affairs. I was a teenager, but I knew that this was one time it was better to be seen than to be heard.

Besides, I couldn't believe the emotions I was seeing on Daddy's face.

He opened his mouth, then closed it as if he'd considered and rejected the words he'd planned to say. His eyes darted toward us and back to Mama, as he realized her love for her kids wouldn't keep her from walking out on him.

"I, I . . . We can talk. . . ."

That wasn't what Mama wanted to hear.

She wanted him to beg, "Don't go," to plead, "Please stay, I'm sorry."

He couldn't do that. He loved her, truly loved her. I could see it in the way his shoulders slumped, the way his body swayed like a fighter determined to stand upright. His emotions bled through his pores. But he couldn't beg.

They loved each other from their own territory. There was no neutral ground, no place to negotiate a truce. There was only victory or defeat.

Mama left. She returned a few days later to a stalemate. She wouldn't give and neither would he.

Mama doesn't like to talk about the way she grieved after Daddy's death.

"You see," she'll say, "Mama didn't cry long, honey. She went out and got her another man."

I was not gentle when I corrected the record. My words were sharp as I pulled out comments and conversations that reminded her of the pain she'd decided to forget. Now, though, I'm older and I understand: she needed the story she crafted to protect herself against her regrets.

"You know," she once admitted, "there were a lot of things I could have done for Max."

She could have mixed his scotch and water, fixed his plate at dinner. She could have been kind without being submissive. It was a thin line, but she could have walked it. And she might have, if he had been able to appreciate the fact that her gestures came from love, not from obligation.

But he couldn't be a better husband, any more than she

could have been a better wife. They couldn't work together because they didn't know how.

They hadn't had fathers. Mama's daddy left the family when
she was a child; she barely spoke to him when she was an adult.
Daddy's father left too, then died. My parents were feeling their
way as husband and wife for most of their relationship.

"You know," Mama said. "Sometimes I go downstairs and
I see Max's car under the carport. And I wonder where he went,
why he didn't wake me up and tell me he was leaving.

"Then I remember. He's gone."

Chapter Four

When I was sixteen, just weeks away from college and freedom, I'd made a vow to a neighbor. I'd stood at the edge of the patio, full in the sun, disdaining the comfort of the carport. My neighbor wasn't as brave. She faced me, holding her hand to her eyes to protect them from the glare.

"Christie, when I leave here, I ain't ever coming back."

She stepped forward, as if the light had impaired her hearing as well as her vision. But I had declared my independence as firmly as Patrick Henry had shouted his preference for liberty or death.

College had been my way out. They had all attended Tennessee State. I chose the University of Chicago, for the city as much as the school. I ran as far away as they would let a sixteen-year-old go.

Twelve years had passed since that conversation, but Christie hadn't forgotten about it. She looked at me, seeing a woman leaving her twenties and heading into her thirties, and thought I'd broken my vow.

"Well you came back," she said.

"Yeah, for a minute," I joked, but I meant it. I was visiting, not staying.

She'd strolled over to check out the unfamiliar yellow car parked on the patio. Or maybe she'd seen me pulling my bags out of the trunk, and wondered who was helping me. I'd known Christie most of my life; she moved two doors away just weeks after we'd settled in.

Really, my brother had discovered the family. Tired of playing with his sisters, he'd left the house in search of friends. A few hours later, he returned with another little boy in tow. Christie's kids were younger than I, so I drifted toward her. She was like the older sister or the sympathetic aunt I'd needed so badly during my teenaged years.

She looked at the car and at me, smiling and reprising the conversation from so many years ago. "You said you were never coming back here."

And I'd kept my part of the bargain. She'd squinted at Stephanie Odelia Scruggs, the kid whose feet could hardly stand to stay still. She would never return. I'd changed my name just weeks before my visit. I'd become Afi-Odelia Efuru Scruggs. I was here not out of homesickness, but to introduce myself to my family.

The name wasn't a mystery to them. I'd received it during my first year of graduate school. It was a curiosity, as exotic as the language I studied—and, in their opinion, just about as useful.

"You don't know what you want to be," my father declared when I told him about my naming ceremony.

"Not true! I know what I am."

I was a prospective college professor, on my way to the ivory tower. The who of my identity, though, was up for grabs. I'd known that Stephanie Odelia Scruggs could no longer contain my spirit. The name was no longer unique enough to fit the woman I would be.

I was told that Afi Efuru meant "Spiritual Daughter of Heaven." Those five syllables promised infinite potential. I'd worn the name informally for seven years, inhabiting its contours until, finally, I could present it to the world.

Christie walked over to the car, nodding in approval. She stroked it quickly, afraid the hot metal would scorch her fingers. I stretched my legs and arm, following behind her as she circled the car. I measured how I'd fit in a home, a neighborhood, and a way of life that, despite my father's death, seemed to have remained static while I'd charged ahead.

I gave half my attention to the conversation. With the other half, I composed the speech announcing that I'd discarded the name my parents had labored over for nine months.

"So you got a car now?"

"Yep, a stick shift."

I'd parked my Japanese economy car at the edge of the patio, behind Daddy's Lincoln and Mama's Cadillac. Those cars didn't leave much room for another, but my sedan could fight for the tightest corner. Yet the giant vehicles resting underneath the carport didn't overwhelm it. Its size took visitors by surprise. The Scruggses were known for their luxury cars.

My family bought automobiles that matched their personalities. I joined them on that score. My car was just like me, compact and simple, but different enough from the expected to pull one closer. I'd wanted a car the color of a robin's egg, or a clear summer sky. I waited for weeks until, frustrated, I bought the canary yellow car. When I parked it, I almost laughed out loud. I had a car, my car, my way of getting wherever I wanted to go. I locked the door and walked away, turning with every step to admire my new declaration of independence.

I had my door key in hand when my smile got even bigger. I was glad the car was yellow. All of my mother's cars had been blue.

"You didn't get an automatic transmission?"

"Stick shifts are cheaper and better on gas."

My parents' cars were trophies they'd earned after years of doing without and straining to make ends meet. Little by little they accumulated their rewards: the two-story white brick colonial; my father's B.S. in accounting; my mother's master's degree; children who walked out of college and into professional jobs. Their cars advertised their accomplishments and position. Wherever they went, people would know that they had money to burn in the tanks of their monstrous vehicles.

I wasn't there yet, if ever I would be. My mother had taught me how to budget when I was still in elementary school. Once a month she handed over twenty dollars. She watched as I bent over my sheet of paper, stretching the money to cover a month of bus tokens, school lunches, and church contributions. The lesson carried me through the lean years of college and a graduate stipend of two hundred dollars a month. I wasn't a miser, but I respected and feared money. I felt safest with a roof over my head, and clothes on my back, and quite a few dollars in a savings account.

"You drove all the way from Virginia by yourself? How many hours was that, ten, twelve?"

I grinned. The entire conversation was a prelude to this question. I thought about turning monosyllabic, then reconsidered. Christie had been my listening ear throughout high school. Her oldest child had been my brother's first friend. One thing I'd learned from my mother: always pay your debts.

"No, my boyfriend, Robert, helped me out."

* * *

When my father died, I promised myself I would avoid love. I saw myself as others saw me, vulnerable and grieving. I was barely able to contain my pain and longing. I didn't want to attach to someone else.

So I immediately tumbled into one relationship, then another and a third. The last fall was the hardest and furthest.

I wasn't looking for a surrogate father. I just wanted someone to hold, someone to stand beside. I'd dammed my love and stored it for the future. I wanted to open the gates and let it flow in all its abundance. The first two men got a relative trickle that dried up when the affairs faltered and failed.

The last almost drowned in the flood.

His name was Robert.

His courteousness brought us together. I was walking up the street, lugging a television to my apartment in Charlottesville. I'd become so accustomed to frugality as a graduate student, the eighteen thousand dollars I now earned as an assistant professor didn't entice me into extravagance. I knew I needed a car, so I started saving toward a down payment. Until then, I walked.

Somehow I'd gotten a small black-and-white set; knowing me, I'd discovered a bargain at the Goodwill. I trudged up the hill from campus to my high rise, so intent on my destination and my prize that I didn't hear the man come up behind me.

I almost dropped the set when he spoke to me.

He offered to carry it, and I handed it over gladly. My blood was still thick and sluggish, and September in Virginia felt like a hot, sticky, New England July. Sweat rolled down my arms, which ached from my load. I was happy to let someone else carry it. If this good-looking man was a thief, well, that was a television gone. I'd cry over it when I got home to my air conditioner.

If he'd been a thief, I could have given police a detailed description. I simply couldn't look at anything else other than the man walking beside me.

His skin was deep brown with a red undertone that gave his complexion a warm glow. His short hair barely covered a head that looked like a sculptor had labored to create a balanced, symmetrical oval. His teeth shone white and strong against his skin.

He could have the television. He could have me, if he wanted.

"What's your name?" I had the presence of mind to ask that question. If I didn't know his name, how would I find him again?

He told me, and asked for mine.

"Afi," I said, even though I wouldn't legally claim the name for another nine months. I'd been Afi for five years by then, and the name change would be just a formal announcement of my new identity. Besides, Stephanie wouldn't have been lusting after a man she'd just met. Stephanie would have politely declined his help and walked home as fast as the cumbersome television would allow.

We swapped histories. I rolled out my credentials: a Slavic linguist, researching English language acquisition by Russian immigrants. He looked at me, digesting the kernel I'd given him to swallow.

"Isn't that . . . obscure?" He'd paused before asking, but it didn't soften the question.

"Well, what do you do?"

He was an undergraduate, interested in engineering.

"And Slavic linguistics is obscure?" I laughed.

He grinned and handed me the television. He was too much of a gentleman to see me to my door. After all, he was a stranger.

"Thank you," I said, not only for the help but also for the decorum. I didn't want him to know where I lived.

Yet.

Late that night, I turned off the air conditioner and opened the sliding glass door. The warm breeze carried the scent of my night blooming jasmine throughout the apartment. I breathed deeply as I cut off the lights. I sat on my couch in the darkness and silence, listening to the lingering melody of a stranger's voice.

Robert reminded me of my father. That was not a distinguishing characteristic. All my boyfriends were like my father. But Robert shared more traits than the others.

Robert was what my father could have been, would have been, had he been born into a life filled with advantages instead of obstacles. Robert was intelligent and intellectual, passionately defending blacks while moving in spheres mostly populated by whites. My father called it the "fly in the buttermilk" syndrome—a lonely speck of color treading in a sea of whiteness. Daddy had come to some acceptance of his destiny, could even laugh about it. Robert hadn't evolved far enough to see the ironic humor in his circumstances. He was young, still energetic enough to go to war on a moment's notice instead of measuring his battles; too naive to understand the necessity of a strategic retreat.

The truth was he was a middle-class black man, the child of doting parents. He was fortunate to have been born after, not during, the inevitable destruction of segregation. He was a child of his generation, receiving the gifts that blacks had struggled since Reconstruction to obtain.

During segregation, a black person at the University of Virginia was sure to be a janitor or a maid. In fact, the state had sent black public school teachers wanting advanced degrees to Harvard rather than integrate its precious "University." Robert knew how much it had taken for blacks to walk through campus holding books instead of brooms—and I think he felt guilty.

His privilege was a burden he wore gladly, pushing to prove his mettle as a black man to society as well as to himself. My father had come to some acceptance of that load, too. He'd learned to shift it from shoulder to shoulder, when to rest, when to carry on—and when to admit defeat.

Those lessons came with age and, I'm convinced, a life of little or nothing. Robert had experienced neither. I loved him for his potential, the power I saw waiting to be unleashed, the ardor and strength that roiled below his deceptively placid demeanor. So I made the mistake that lovers always make: I assumed that the world would see what I saw and feel all I felt. I took Robert home to my mother, confident she would share my vision.

She took one look at him and saw the traits that would break my heart over and over. His eyes stared down the bridge of his straight nose before returning to her face. His mouth settled into a line so tightly sealed that it almost refused to open and say hello. He shook his head over the dark purple bathroom and the paint peeling from the ceiling. Makeup, jewelry, and bills covered every flat surface. He recoiled from the ostentatious shabbiness, seeing, I felt, laziness instead of a woman still feeling her way through a new life after twenty-seven years of negotiating an old one.

He was mounting his defenses against the force of her personality. Mama didn't just inhabit her house. She ruled it, enforcing her edicts like a queen. Daddy's death had left her lonely, and she filled the void the way she'd always done, gathering people around her, helping them by pouring her efforts into their lives until she had nothing left to give.

Robert's parents were taciturn. Quiet and decorum reigned in their home. During the entire length of our relationship, almost three years, I never dropped by his house without calling. He'd never told me, but I knew such a liberty wasn't allowed.

At my mother's, the telephone began to ring each morning at five. The chimes at the back door played "Big Ben" constantly, announcing relatives and friends who filled the house. Visitors lounged on the beds and watched television. They plopped down on the carpet, pushing aside piles of books and kicking stray shoes back under the bed. When they left, radios and television played softly throughout the night.

Managing the chaos left little time to contemplate the reality of life without my father. Mama had faced the emptiness of her grief and fled, frightened, into the comfort of clutter and noise.

Robert had no weapons against such a psychic and emotional onslaught. He protected his space by retreating into aloofness. My father had used the same weapon. But my mother loved my father. Robert was a stranger, invading her territory.

Every conversation was a challenge. Small greetings were pro forma, not sincere. Their battle lines were drawn and there could be no truce. Once again, I was in the middle. So I retreated. I took Robert and headed for the state archives.

Chapter Five

Libraries have always been my refuge. The silence and single-mindedness of the patrons creates a comforting sense of isolation and timelessness. In a library, I am guaranteed the right to settle down and lose myself in whatever I feel like doing—writing, knitting, maybe staring off into space. I'm able to *be*, without worrying about laziness.

When I walked into the Tennessee State Library and Archives, I paused a second and detached myself from the world on the other side of the heavy glass doors. My excitement rose from my stomach to my chest. I gasped, hoping the short breaths would slow down my heart.

I would find something, I was sure of it. What, I didn't know. Still, even a small tear in the veil surrounding my family's history would be sufficient. Any hole could be enlarged. Pushing and pulling would ultimately rip the curtain enough to give me a full view of my ancestral past. It might take a while, possibly three years. Eventually I'd know who we were.

"Have you ever been here before?" The librarian knew the answer before I shook my head; I'd asked to see the 1920 census.

The census information is released after seventy-two years, the librarian explained. I was a decade too early. He pulled out a worn notebook.

"This is the Soundex," he said, introducing me to that vital name index.

The Soundex is a code of letters and numbers assigned to surnames. The process is simple, but expansive enough to account for all the twists of family names. After a couple of false starts, I figured out the code, S620, and located the microfilm for the 1910 census.

I claimed a machine large enough for Robert and me. I'd brought a few pieces of paper, not even a notebook, and a pencil. Too late, I realized how meager my preparations were. But the microfilm was threaded and the past was waiting to be unwound. I leaned toward the screen, losing myself in the lists of generations long dead, escaping from family still alive.

I could have gone straight for my grandfather's name: William Henry Scruggs, black, living in Williamson County, Tennessee. The basic bits of information were just enough to lead me to him if he was listed in the Soundex. But I wanted to wade into the pool of names and lives contained on the reel.

"Help me," I told Robert. "You look at the race and I'll look at the county." With a turn of a reel, I abandoned the present for the past.

The census tells the story of a community by revealing the lives of its individual residents: whether it was a crossroads where farmers came to trade, or a town with merchants and lawyers; whether the women labored in the fields beside their husbands and children, or kept orderly homes for others more prosperous than they.

But the Soundex lacks the richness of the census proper. It is merely a list, divorced from any social or cultural context, devoid of any history other than the meager facts given for each entry. It would reveal my grandfather's whereabouts in 1910, and who lived with him. It would tell his age and the names of his parents—if they were still alive.

I could have gone straight to the end of the microfilm, looking for William Scruggs—or better yet, his father Washington. But I was a miner, chipping and sifting for precious nuggets that might accumulate value later in my research.

We trolled through the names slowly, lingering over anyone who was black, no matter where he or she lived.

Sharpes, Sawyers, an occasional Searcy. Both Robert and I were students of our history. We understood that the blacks on those rolls were a generation or two out of slavery—if that. Their existence was a victory over a system that had denied them the assurance of their family's survival. Mothers hugged fathers, siblings and cousins kissed, all knowing the embraces could be their last. Yet not even fifty years later, sons had become fathers, and fathers had become grandfathers. Their lives were fading into reminiscences told to uncomprehending children.

Our eyes were tired. Our necks had begun to ache. Still we turned the reel, stopping at the name of a black Scruggs—any black Scruggs—living in Williamson County. We went through name after name, even though I knew that names were insufficient. I wanted feelings: the joy of looking at one's descendants, certain that they would never be sold away from you; the confidence of knowing that your life belonged to you, not to some master or mistress; the exhilaration of realizing that the chain which had shackled your children before their very conception had, miraculously, been severed.

William C. Scruggs, Harden Cty. White. William C. Scruggs, Greene Cty. White. William C. Scruggs, Fayette Cty. Black.

William Scruggs, Williamson Cty. Black. Born March 12, 1898. Head of household. Enumerated with Dick Scruggs.

"My grandfather!"

The exclamation flew from my mouth so quickly that I almost forgot to whisper.

"We've found my grandfather!"

I wasn't sure. I'd left the list of births and deaths somewhere, my mother's house or even in Virginia. I brushed aside my doubts and stepped out on faith, the substance of all I'd hope to find.

My quick calculations reassured me. The evidence was indeed before my eyes. This child would have been in his thirties around 1929, when my father was born. He would have been young enough and strong enough to help conceive six children. This William Scruggs had to be my grandfather.

But who was Dick Scruggs?

I asked Aunt Helen. "I never heard that name."

PART TWO

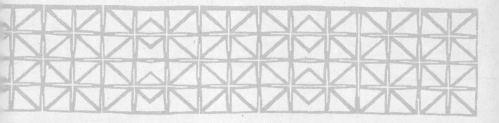

PART TWO

Chapter Six

I'd started looking for Scruggses whenever and wherever I could, crossing my fingers that unlikely venues would lead me to a mother lode of information. My serendipitous battle had been unsuccessful. But I'd been so estranged from my family's history that I believed anything I needed could come at any time, through miraculous ways.

So when I stepped into the genealogy reading room at the library in Philadelphia, Mississippi, I sent a silent prayer to God and my ancestors.

"Lead me, guide me," I begged. "If something is here, show it to me."

Work, not pleasure, had brought me to this little town in east Mississippi. My joy at being a college professor quickly changed to a feeling of constriction. Charlottesville was a beautiful place, but it was a small town in the Blue Ridge Mountains. The geography hemmed me in; going to Richmond was a big thrill.

The Slavic department was small and tightly knit. I was a temporary hire, lured there with the promise of a shot at a full-time job. I knew I'd lost out when a candidate from California

delivered her lecture. Afterwards, while I was waiting to introduce myself, I heard her ask the chairman about housing and
moving expenses. At twenty-eight, I could accept another temporary teaching job, or get out of the field altogether.

It had taken four years for me to figure out what I wanted
to do. I was as surprised as my family when I ended up as a
reporter. I was as shocked as my mother when I got my first
full-time job at a daily paper.

"Well, I'll be damned," she said when she learned I'd be
going to Jackson, Mississippi.

I was a reporter for the state's largest newspaper: the black
reporter with the African name, working for a paper that had
fought the good fight for segregation. I was writing a retrospec-
tive on "Freedom Summer."

I was the first of several journalists who would descend
upon Philadelphia in June 1989. It was a rite. Every five years,
reporters returned to write about one of the most horrible slay-
ings of the civil rights era: the deaths of Andrew Goodman,
James Chaney, and Mickey Schwerner.

The three civil rights workers had been waylaid and brutally
beaten. Federal law enforcement officers searched for weeks, until a tip led them to decomposed remains buried in an earthen
dam. Close to twenty men had been involved in the conspiracy.
They were never tried for murder, a state crime. Their only punishment was federal convictions for obstructing the victims' civil
rights.

The blacks in town nodded in grim satisfaction when the
journalists arrived. The sins of the past would be exhumed one
more time. Whites girded themselves and sealed their lips. They
knew the deed would be forgotten.

One day.

Reporters found themselves caught in currents of race and

resentment. They painted the town in broad strokes, and got out. I had arrived two months before the anniversary of the murders. I moved in with a black woman on the other side of the tracks. I went to church. I ate at the small cafes that passed for restaurants. Still I had my limits. I never went to the movies. Blacks sat in the balcony, gazing over the heads of the whites seated below. It was the custom.

Yet the town was beautiful. The wisterias shimmered after the springtime rains. In the morning, they tinted the fog, turning the mist into a collection of pastels.

I drove cautiously, slowly negotiating the curving roads of eastern Mississippi, pondering the serenity of this place. I rolled my window down, inhaling the perfume of flowers and freshly turned earth. East Mississippi was as rural as the Delta, but the ground there was a lush red, deep as the skins of the Choctaws who had stubbornly clung to the land they had claimed for generations. They seemed to come from the earth that had been plowed so carefully, anticipating the end of the rains and the beginning of planting. Each furrow seemed a scar, a reminder that the ground had willingly accepted the corpses of three innocent men.

When the oppression became too burdensome, I hid in the county library. I snuggled deep in an armchair, escaping the strain of constant observation and questioning by losing myself in the pages of a book.

Or I browsed the genealogy room, researching local families to ease my guilt over my attempts to escape my surroundings. I pulled out the books of chattel contracts, trying to see how black and white lives had been intertwined.

Through it all, I kept an eye open for Scruggses. I didn't expect to find anything, but my short stint as a reporter had taught me an important lesson: I could find a needle in a haystack, if I was patient and tenacious enough to sift through every bit of straw.

It was natural, then, that I'd notice the small green hardback with "Tennessee" in its title. The book wasn't out of place. The two states shared a border, and many Mississippians had roots there. I flipped to the index and noted the listings for Young and Theodorick Scruggs of Williamson County.

"There were lots of Scruggses in Williamson County," I told myself. "Maybe this will lead to something."

I badly needed the names of white people if I was to reach past the 1870 census. In order to locate my family, I'd eventually need records left by their owners—provided those records survived, or had even been kept in the first place. Young and Theodorick might turn to be just who I'd been looking for.

"Nothing beats a blank but a try," I recited. I started with the listing for Young; I liked his name best.

His father, Edward, had migrated west from Virginia. His mother, Alpha Hassell, had come from North Carolina. The couple had nine children: John, William, Ed, Nancy . . . , Young, Theodorick . . . The family's life was thrown into turmoil when Edward died without a will. . . .

I sat down, reading the brightly written passages again and again. I took notes, then read some more. I turned to the passage on Theodorick. It repeated Young's.

I automatically started thinking like a reporter. If Ed Scruggs died suddenly, he might not have left a will. All his assets—his house, his land, his slaves—would have been tallied for the probate hearing. If the document survived, I might have a shot at tracking down my relatives.

There I was, miles away from Tennessee, in a city trying to erase its history, and I'd stumbled upon my own.

"Thank you," I said softly, grateful to God and the ancestors who must have led me here.

"Thank you," to Ed Scruggs, whose existence I'd doubted, to the anonymous insurance agent who'd handed my mother the names I'd just confirmed.

"Thank you," to any and all the forces that had helped me. My standard had been met. The information in the book put my skepticism to rest. I was humbled and so joyful that I overlooked the larger, darker significance of my discovery.

For the past six years, I'd been looking for people. From now on, I'd be searching for property.

I'd never had to consider the mundane inhumanity of slavery—which meant I'd never confronted the reality of the institution—until I stood in the Williamson County courthouse, struggling to fit a huge, dusty volume on the top of a copier.

My mother's family, the keeper of our stories, did not talk about slavery. In their creation myth, we were the offspring of whites and Cherokees. My skin was dark and my hair was kinky because of intermarriage with others who had less stellar bloodlines. Still, my color didn't contradict the family lore. My red undertone pointed to my Indian heritage. Society called us "Negroes" in spite of our straight hair and blue-gray eyes. But that misnomer was a trick of fate; slavery had no part in our history.

Make no mistake, though, I knew about slavery. My grandmother and mother were teachers. Each February, they pulled out pictures and decorations for "Negro History Week." My racial pride wasn't built on stories of African kings and queens. I'd learned about George Washington Carver's trek to the Missouri school, which denied him entrance when they saw his face. I'd heard the Reverend Martin Luther King Jr. speak. I passed Fisk University each Sunday on my way to church.

I was raised in the South, if not born there. I knew who built the fabulous plantations that whites folks claimed for their heritage. I knew who broke ground and planted the crops, who put the money in the masters' pockets. I didn't hesitate to proclaim that I was the descendant of slaves.

The claim took on a more intimate and powerful meaning when I found the books of county court proceedings. There, among the documents, I found filings after filings settling the estate of Ed Scruggs.

Appraisers cataloged his estate in 1847, right after he died. "Inventory of the property of Edward Scruggs, dec., prepared for the June term of the county court for 1847," the document began, ". . . seven beds and bedsteads, two small looking glasses . . . one set of tea ware containing 6–8 pieces. . . .

The accounting continued: "1 pair waffle irons, 2 washing tubs, one waggon [sic] one carriage, eleven plows, one grinding hoe . . . twelve head of horses & mules one yoke oxen eighteen head of cattle . . .

"Also the Following Negroes, viz. Lynda and her children. . . .

I found my grandfather in this section, enumerated with "Eliza and her 9 children, Abe, Dick Anthony, Adam, George, Charles, Amanda, Jerry and Eliza."

The slaves were divided again in 1850, when a group of them—along with several parcels of land—were placed in trust for Ed Scruggs's minor heirs. I found Dick again; he was appraised at five hundred and fifty dollars.

These pages were the keys to my family's origins, and I wanted them badly. Although I'd been a full-time journalist just

a few years, I'd learned to ask for whatever I wanted. Sometimes, many times, I got it.

"Can you help me," I said, politely, almost humbly ap-
proaching the office manager. "I need to make a copy of these
pages."

She opened the gate into the business side of the office, and
waited while I carefully arranged the book on the glass plate.

"I'm so excited," I said, checking to make sure all the meticulous writing would fit onto a reduced page. "I'm doing genealogy, looking in these records, and I think I just found my
great-great-grandfather."

The entire office perked up a bit. Now my presence wasn't
obtrusive, but explainable. This thin black woman who had interrupted their routine may have been a stranger. But she wasn't
an outsider.

"Where do you live?" she asked.

"In Mississippi now. I'm a reporter. My father's side was
from here."

"What's your name?"

"I'm a Scruggs." I strained to close the cover of the copier
over the top of the book. "My relatives belonged to a man
named Ed Scruggs. He died without a will. I found an inventory
of his estate, and all his slaves are listed."

Did the mention of slavery add a chill to the conversation?
I didn't care. I refused to evade the facts of the past. Plus, I'd
brought the lines of my family an inch closer.

I glanced up to meet the gaze of a black office worker. "You
know better," her expression seemed to say. "You know we
don't talk about things like this around white people."

I smiled, shrugged, and turned back to the office manager.
"How much do I owe? For the copies?"

Her boss took over.

"Don't worry about them," he said. "They're on us."

Chapter Seven

For much of my life, I thought my family began with my father. He was, after all, the only Scruggs I knew.

Aunt Helen was a Prime, and Aunt Irene was a Thomas. They *had* been Scruggses, but that was a long time ago, before my birth. When I was growing up, a woman took her husband's name without question, relinquishing her personal identity to become part of her mate's. My aunts and cousins never felt like Scruggses to me, but relatives.

My grandmother Dodo wasn't a Scruggs either. I considered her an Aiden.

All of the paternal relatives I knew came from her side of the family: my aunts Estella and Regener; Jennie and Ida; my uncles Henry and Willard. They belonged to a complex clump of full and half-siblings whose father was "Daddy" Henry Aiden. He'd had several wives—family lore said two, the census and other records said four—but all his children stood together under his surname.

My paternal grandfather was a ghost of a grandparent, as shadowy as his oldest son and namesake. There were no Scruggses in my life besides my father and his children.

Daddy stood tall as the head of the family, even when his nephews grew up to look him in his eye, or look down at the top of his head. He was their only uncle, Max. He was the man in the family.

I'm sure my father saw himself this way. He was dedicated to the notion of generations branching out from a common trunk. His brother had died too young to have children. His sisters were married; their children wore other names. My father did his duty by siring three children, including a son. If my brother cooperated, our branch of Scruggses would sprout another generation.

The feminist in me rebelled at Daddy's sexism. I could carry on the family name as well as my brother. "Just give me nine months," I told Daddy, "and I can give you some Scruggses."

"Do you want them light-skinned or dark-skinned, half white or all black? Put your order in."

Daddy didn't appreciate my sarcasm, or the allusion to my interracial relationship. "You shouldn't talk to your Daddy that way," he said. "You're gonna miss me when I'm gone."

But he didn't understand how much I loved being a Scruggs. I loved the way my tongue bunched up in my mouth when I pronounced the hard consonants, and how the air escaped from my mouth when I started and ended my name. Feminism had given me permission to remain a Scruggs, whether married or single, and I intended to do just that.

When Daddy died, I knew I'd never change my mind. My surname reminded me of him. I could sign my name and see my father covering my cheeks with wet, runny kisses when I was a little girl. My first name had been changed, and might be changed again. But my last name would always testify to my standing as Max Scruggs's daughter, the oldest of three children, and the first baby he held in his arms.

When I found Dick Scruggs, though, I saw a lineage that included my father instead of originating with him. The Scruggses had length: Daddy was the fourth generation from Dick and I was the fifth.

I copied the names of Dick's children from the census—Charles, Henry, Emma, Dosia, and Julia—and considered their children. I hadn't known our family had such breadth. I studied the estate documents carefully, growing more and more familiar with the precise script that had preserved my heritage. A host of names preceded my great-great grandfather's name; another list followed it. The Scruggs plantation was more than a white man's estate. It was a community of families, rooted in and defined by geography.

My notion of my identity began to transcend my obsession with my father. Maybe this was time doing its healing; Daddy had been dead at least three years when I came upon Dick Scruggs. My father was still important to me, but he wasn't the definitive figure he'd been when I'd begun my investigation.

Dick Scruggs showed me that the Scruggses were not a straight line, as I'd first assumed. We were a mass of sisters and brothers, doing double duty as cousins, uncles, and aunts; sons and daughters; mothers and fathers.

We were a growing organism that, somehow, encompassed my family.

Chapter Eight

I gleaned a little about Dick from the documents I found. I didn't build my profile from notes or comments. The slaves were grouped in families, listed by name, and appraised. Dick was valued at five hundred and fifty dollars.

He was young in 1847, probably in his late teens, but certainly no older than twenty-one or twenty-two. He was strong enough to work in his master's fields, not his house. If he had been much older, he probably would have been worth less—unless he was a carpenter or a blacksmith. Then his market price would have increased by several hundred dollars, or even doubled. The valuation, the date of the will, all of those numbers added up to this inescapable conclusion: Dick had always been a slave, and would have died one had fate not intervened.

In the beginning Dick's enslavement was academic to me, perhaps because I'd never known of his existence. When I discovered his name on the census, he was a free man. But the inventories gave him shape and form. I began to feel the chronology of his life, to imagine him hiding during the Civil War's battle of Franklin. Where, I wondered, had he been when he'd gotten word of his liberty? What had he done? Had the Klan raids and the backlash of Reconstruction embittered him, or left him longing for Ned Scruggs's protection?

Mostly I wondered how Dick looked. Had any part of him been reincarnated in my father?

Africans believe the ancestors reincarnate in pieces: a child might wear the father's features; a grandchild might carry his disposition; a niece or nephew imitate his walk and talk. I was working backwards, reconstructing an ancestor from the pictures I had of my grandfather and my father.

My father's features informed my own. I gazed at myself in the mirror many times after he died, comforting myself that, no matter what had happened, I'd see my father in the contours of my face. I wore his thick, full lips. I shared his poor eyesight.

And my feet were big, just like his.

"You even walk like him," a stranger once exclaimed. The man had stared at me five full minutes before getting up the courage to leave his seat. "I'm sorry, you look like someone but he's dead." I didn't need to ask whom he meant; I knew. His comment warmed my grief, like a thick blanket on a cold dreary day. But my father looked like his mother, Dora Aiden. I knew the Scruggses best from a torn picture of my grandfather, my grandmother, and their first child.

My grandfather William was not as tall as my father, who was only 5'9" or 5'10". But my father had long limbs, as if his torso had not reached the potential promised by his arms and legs. His bones were small and deceptively delicate for a man. The little fat that cushioned his frame came much later, when the discipline of his military routine had given way to days in an office, and nights dozing on the couch in his den.

My grandfather was thick, the family portrait showed that much. His shoulders were broad. He wasn't yellow, but light enough. His wife was darker, with a rich, opaquely brown complexion. Her hair was neatly pulled back to render the kinky strands as inoffensive as possible.

But my grandfather's short, sculptured hair fell in crisp waves from the top of his head to the nape of his neck. His complexion and hair texture alone made him a prize. Any woman would have been proud to rest her hand on his arm and match her stride with his.

The portrait wasn't a framed picture, but a postcard sent back to relatives in Nashville. My grandparents hadn't been married two years before the baby arrived. They named her Katherine, after her great-grandmother, I believe. Hers was just one of the names that would travel through generations, pointing the way to unfamiliar relatives.

Young and recently married, with a baby on the way, they picked up and moved to Detroit in 1920. My grandmother planned to go to mortuary school. My grandfather's goals have been lost.

Maybe he had none.

Maybe he simply wanted to stretch his arms without hitting the obstacles that pinned blacks down South. Detroit was a promise, like candy after church.

There a black man's reach could extend all the way to his fingers. There he could flex his muscles and test himself. There success was not a threat to the whites whose need for control hobbled a young man's hopes. My grandparents joined millions of other blacks who lifted their eyes and gazed north, to Chicago, to Cleveland, to Detroit.

The postcard was their proof. They'd made it. Their child would be the first of a new generation. She would take deep, confident breaths. She would never learn to measure the weight and consequences of her words before opening her mouth.

But reality eroded their aspirations. My grandmother was

carrying a second baby even while she stood with her husband and their first. The postcard heralded their new year of dreams. It would mock them by Christmas, when she lay on her bed in Nashville, nursing their first son.

My father was his mother's son. His sister, Irene, was her father's daughter. If the Scruggses had passed down any trait, it was their short, stocky stature. I needed more for my great-great-grandfather. I wanted the sound of his voice, the color of his eyes, the way his hands moved when he played with the grand-children that filled his yard.

Desperately, I turned back to Aunt Helen. She had no answers to share, but she sent me to someone else. She gave me the name of a cousin, Edna, who listened while I introduced myself.

"I know who you are." Her voice fluttered with age. "You need to call Bertha Brown."

*Wedding picture of the author's parents, Max Walter Scruggs Sr. and
Irene Elizabeth Daniel Scruggs, May 19, 1952*

Family of Max Walter Scruggs Jr. and Metrice Scruggs (the author's brother and sister-in-law), December 1989. From left rear: Max Walter Scruggs Jr.; Enrica Covington, daughter; Sapriya Scruggs, daughter; Max Walter Scruggs III, son; Metrice Scruggs, holding Bakari Ali Scruggs, son

The author and her sister as children. From left:
Afi-Odelia E. Scruggs, Jennifer Scruggs

The author and her mother and maternal grandmother, 1996.
From left front: Afi-Odelia E. Scruggs, Irene Elizabeth Daniel Scruggs Midgett,
and Mary Elizabeth Moor Daniel Evans

Katherine Louise Scruggs, the author's maternal aunt

Portrait of the Scruggs family, 1921. From left: Dora Louise Aiden Scruggs (paternal grandmother); William Henry Scruggs Sr. (paternal grandfather), holding Katherine Louise Scruggs

Irene Elizabeth Daniel Scruggs, 1960

Max Walter Scruggs Sr., 1968

Chapter Nine

I gazed at the woman sitting across from me, trying to find my features in her face. She was my Cousin Bertha, the link to generations I'd come to know through records and documents.

Her skin was light brown, the same color as the sweetened milk strengthened with a tablespoon of coffee I'd tasted as a little girl. I'd begged for the drink, desperate to imitate the adults who sipped and sighed their way into wakefulness. "No," Elizabeth answered. "Children don't drink coffee." But I nagged and whined, assaulting her defenses until she capitulated and fixed me a cup—with a warning.

"Black coffee will make you black."

She looked me in the eye. I held her gaze, surprising us both with my assertiveness. Children didn't confront adults in thought, word, or deed back then. But I knew if I held firm, her mouth would twitch, and her eyebrow would lift. Something would happen to confirm that she was lying.

She didn't flinch. She was so practiced in the art of pulling my leg, she knew she could outwit my small attempt to find her out. She kept her eyes on me, not saying a word until curiosity defeated her resolve.

"What are you doing?"

I'd added a stream of evaporated milk to my coffee, and my cup came close to running over. I started off imitating Grandma Moore. But in that instant, I realized I'd found my weapon.

"If black coffee makes you black, then light coffee makes you light. Right?"

My grandmother rolled her eyes and got up from the table. I added two more tablespoons of sugar to the cup. My drink was as sweet as my victory.

Light coffee would never bleach my skin to the color of the woman sitting in front of me now. It would never untwist my kinky hair so that its texture matched hers. My skin would remain as dark as the coffee my father had perked every morning.

The smell enticed me out of my dreams, an aromatic alarm more effective than the radios that blared before sunrise. Daddy didn't have much use for cups. He drank from a white, chipped mug he filled just short of the brim, so the coffee wouldn't spill on his pristine shirt.

His recipe required two teaspoons of sugar. His palate was so refined he complained when I carelessly skimped and stirred in a teaspoon and a half. His day always began with coffee, eggs, and potatoes, rarely grits, alternately bacon or sausage and, more often than not, toast. That kind of diet kept meat on Daddy's bones, sustaining him as the cigarettes he craved soiled his lungs until they were as black as the coffee that bubbled frantically on the stove.

My complexion linked me to my father as surely as it separated me from my mother's family. When we all gathered at Aunt Helen's for barbecue or baked chicken, I counted the shades of brown among us. My cousin, Kenneth, was jet black; his skin gleamed like it had absorbed light and released it through his pores. Charles, his younger brother, was the shade of purest coffee, uncut with milk or sugar.

My brother was the lightest of us all, but I shrugged that off. My mother's genes had to assert themselves in one of her children. In this crew, he was the exception, not us.

Or so I thought, until I saw Cousin Bertha.

She was a Scruggs and a Brown as well, as close to my grandfather as a sibling, both by blood and association. Their mothers had been sisters, and their fathers, brothers. She knew me from a long time ago, even though I was seeing her for the first time.

When I'd talked to Cousin Edna, I struggled over how to introduce myself.

"Should I say I'm Max Scruggs's daughter?"

"No," Edna said, redefining my identity by lengthening my lineage. "Tell her you're William's granddaughter. I'll tell what she's gonna say. . . ."

"William," Cousin Bertha had repeated.

"Yes Ma'am," I answered, as politely as a well-bred child speaking to a deaconess on Communion Sunday. "Do you re-member . . . ?"

"I know William." She cut me short; annoyed that I'd even thought she would need a reminder. "We was raised up to-gether."

No, she didn't resemble my father or me. When I looked at her, I saw my grandfather.

He stood "low to the ground," my Aunt Helen said. Cousin Bertha barely made it to my shoulder, and I am just five feet, three inches. "People shrink as they age," I told myself. But her delicate frame insisted that she had never been much taller than she was then. I clasped her hand carefully, feeling gangly and awkward for the first time in my life.

My grandfather cut his hair close, in deference to his masculinity if not his vanity. But Cousin Bertha's femininity demanded her hair flow as freely as possible. Her head was covered with a bundle of waves that hung past her waist. "How does she keep them out of the way?" I wondered. Perhaps she sensed my puzzlement for, with a practiced gesture, she lifted her hair and held it to the side while she sat down. Then she released it and the strands tumbled down and hid the back of her chair.

Elizabeth would have taken one look at Cousin Bertha and pronounced the verdict: "Indian blood." That was the code phrase for all that my grandmother found beautiful: the light skin; the hair more curly than kinky; the keen nose and lips. My grandmother's family boasted all those traits. She had anticipated a son-in-law who possessed them, too. Instead she got Daddy, skinny and as dark as a country night, with thick lips and a head full of kinky hair.

Elizabeth's mission was to overcome the deficiencies her granddaughters had inherited. She pressed our hair rigorously, pulling the hot comb until the strands capitulated and hung in limp, shiny submission. She trailed us with a jar of Vaseline, rubbing our limbs to eradicate the fine layer of dry skin we blacks called ash. When she finished, she would smile. "You look three shades lighter with your hair pressed," she exclaimed. "And you have that lovely red undertone. It's your Indian blood."

That so-called Indian blood annoyed me as much as it comforted my grandmother. I was thirteen when I decided to wear my "bad hair" naturally, in a soft halo around my face. I was black and proud to be a Scruggs.

Just like Cousin Bertha.

How old was she then, eighty-nine or ninety? Yet her voice

didn't tremble. Her memory didn't waver. She looked at me with clear brown eyes, aware that we were sitting in her dining room talking about a past that she remembered as clearly as the events of the day before. She was like a sister to my grandfather. And in telling her story, she illuminated his.

I'll tell you who you are. . . . Your great-grandmother's name was Julia. Your great-grandfather's name was Washington Brown, but they called him Dock. . . . His father's name was Washington Brown and his mother's name was Katie Poynor. . . . Your great-great grandmother's name was Bertha Scruggs, but they called her Bithie. . . .

—Cousin Bertha

As a child, my grandfather probably never questioned his identity or his place in the world. His heritage was inescapable. He never greeted a stranger, never hugged a friend who wasn't related to him in some meandering way. He never took a step on ground that his elders hadn't already walked. My grandfather's vistas were confined to the geography of a plantation that had been home to three generations of white and black Scruggses. Ed Scruggs farmed in Williamson County's District Five. The land was rich enough to support him, his wife, and nine children, as well as his fifty or so slaves.

Changes had come in the form of the Union soldiers carrying news of the Emancipation Proclamation. But freedom hadn't separated the Scruggses from their land. It belonged to them all: the whites who owned it and the blacks who worked it. Thus the blacks had as much right to the surname Scruggs as their masters. It marked everyone who wore it, telling who they were, where they came from, and where they belonged, the same as their given names.

Cousin Bertha was one of two sets of twins. She and her sister had been named for their grandmothers, Katie and Bithie. My grandfather, William Henry, had been named for maternal and paternal uncles. They were Scruggses and Browns, from Scruggses and Browns, Poynors and Hunters, Cannons and Cowans. The surnames revolved to become first names that signaled the origins of another generation. William Henry Scruggs could rest in the assurance of his lineage. He was the son of Julia and Washington. He was a member of a tribe of grandchildren growing under the watchful eye of my great-great-grandfather Dick.

"We called him Pap," Cousin Bertha told me.

Would I call him a patriarch? I'm hesitant to bestow that title. A patriarch sounds too much like a master who manipulated the lives of his progeny, just like Ed Scruggs controlled the lives of his slaves. All I really knew of Dick was his value to his former owner and his worth to his new young masters. No, I wouldn't stretch my knowledge any further than the information Cousin Bertha gave me.

Dick was an old man, with a passel of children and grandchildren. They all lived down around Scruggs Farm, on the banks of the Harpeth River and its tributaries. Some of his children married and left to tend their own families. Julia and her children stayed.

Cousin Bertha answered my questions nonchalantly and efficiently, never straying into the reminiscences I'd hoped for. I could see her searching through memories, peeking into rooms closed up long before I'd come with my notebook and pen. But her route was not a circuitous stroll through almost forgotten events and incidents. She opened a door and measured what lay before her. If she found what I requested, she told me. If not, she turned her back and went on. There were none of the false starts I'd wanted, tentative beginnings that would take me down a hidden road to questions I'd never thought to raise.

She was truly a Scruggs and a Brown, carrying both families' idiosyncrasies as well as their genes. If there had been any talkers among my ancestors, they must have learned to reveal themselves to folks who'd proven their trustworthiness. If the entire family was taciturn, only the most skilled interrogator could prick their reserve. I was just a beginning reporter, still mapping the terrain of questions and answers. I hadn't learned to scale defenses constructed to keep strangers at bay. My pen and notebook, I'm sure, intensified the formality of our meeting. I was William's granddaughter, true. Yet I was just a face to match an unfamiliar voice from the telephone. My questions proved how far removed I was from places and people who constructed the core of her experience. The big dining room table, covered with papers and books, might have been a canyon. Our voices, modulated to the room, couldn't carry far enough to bridge the chasm between us. She was a Scruggs and a Brown. So was I. We were family. We were strangers.

I fiddled with the soft pages of my notebook, separating and turning them one by one. I needed those few seconds to widen the conversation from the narrow confines of information sought and information given.

"All I have is names from the census," I apologized. "What were your uncles' names?"

"Uncle Zank, Uncle Pinkham . . ." she pronounced the Southern way, with an "a" as the first vowel. Or maybe it was "Pankham." ". . . Aunt Dosia, Aunt Ann, Aunt Julia . . ."

My names were official: Henry and Charles. Dosia, Julia, Anna, and Abraham.

"Who was uncle Pinkham?" I wrote "ink" but I said "ank."

Cousin Bertha paused and frowned.

"Was that Uncle Abraham, or Uncle Henry, maybe?"

Pinkham was Henry, she thought. Zank, she didn't know his real name.

"How did they get their nicknames?"

She hunched her shoulders and shook her head.

"Aunt Ann, was her other name Sophia?"

"Yes."

I took the information down, connecting names with arrows to indicate relationships, scribbling comments in the margins and drawing stars beside important items. I was disappointed over my inability to break past niceties, so I settled for constructing a stack of facts. It was all for lack of experience. Getting what I wanted would have been as easy as putting the pencil down on the paper, leaning back into the chair and asking simple questions. "Who do you look like? Which relative did you love the best?"

I looked over my list one last time, reluctant to leave the session with my cousin. I knew I would think of a thousand questions the moment I unlocked the door to my apartment.

"Who was Dora Scruggs?" I'd found her name in the census when I found my grandfather's. She had the same name as my grandmother, but was obviously a different person. Was she a cousin, the daughter of an aunt or uncle?

"She was William's sister." Cousin Bertha answered as easily as if I'd asked her to name her children.

"Which William?"

"Your grandfather William."

I stopped, stunned. "My grandfather William had a sister?"

"Your grandfather William had two sisters. Their names were Dora and Elnora. They were twins."

"What happened to them?"

"They died. One was ten, the other was about fifteen."

When I called Aunt Helen, she was as surprised as I had been. Her father only mentioned an older brother, Jerry. He never talked about girls in the family, not even a twin sister who had the same name as his wife.

Chapter Ten

I was three when my grandmother Dora died.

I was too young to memorize the touch of her hand when she grabbed me and wrapped me in her arms. I cannot reproduce the pitch of her voice when she shouted at the kids overrunning her house. I only remember one place she lived, and that's because Aunt Irene stayed there after Dodo's death. It was a small apartment, at the back and top of another building. We had to climb a steep flight of stairs that seemed endless to me. I took each step carefully. One miss and I'd tumble backwards. Or I might slip through the rungs and fall to my death.

Still, my emotions rise whenever I look at Dodo's portrait. I know the woman who prepared for this occasion.

She had pulled her hair into an orderly bun, picked out her best clothes and bundled the little baby—her first—for the trip to the photographer. Dodo's face says little. Her expression is as neatly arranged as her hair. I know she was a woman of laughter and love, a woman too soft for the world that kneaded her life and twisted her few accomplishments into disappointments.

I know because my mother told me.

"She called you Lola," Mama said. "Don't forget that. . . ."
Lola was a female character in *Damn Yankees*, the ugliest woman
on earth, who had sold her soul for beauty. She was a temptress,
who knew her power and used it. "Whatever Lola wants, Lola
gets. . . ." Dodo used to say while pointing at me.

I was spoiled. She and Elizabeth had seen to that. "Whatever Lola wants, Lola gets," Dodo sang, and reached for whatever I'd just demanded.

Suddenly the mute woman in the photograph seems to
grin, and wink quickly. Her arm leaves her husband's shoulder
and reaches toward my head. I bend slightly so she can finger
the strands that fall over my ears and down my neck.

"She always said you would have a thick head of hair,"
Mama said. "I don't know how she knew that."

"I'd have to work to find enough hair for a barrette."

She worked hard. My baby pictures show a bald-headed
child wearing a poor excuse for a ponytail.

What if my mother had never told me these stories? What
if she'd merely combed my hair instead of marveling over
Dodo's prescience? What if she had not made my grandmother
such a part of my life that I think of her whenever I comb my
hair?

What if my father's pain and guilt overwhelmed his ability
to talk about his brother William?

Spirits shrink and decay as surely as bones turn to dust in
the grave. After all, my grandfather never spoke of his twin sisters, and we lost them.

No, lost is the wrong word; we could not lose what we
never had.

Elnora and Dora were less than names. They never existed
to us, never would have existed if a nosy great-niece hadn't been
meddling in the microfilm.

Their fate was worse than their deaths, because they had no one to carry on their names, much less their genes. They died young, way too young to have husbands and children. Their peers were children themselves, too young to mourn for long. Time closed its mouth and came close to swallowing them whole.

I don't think my grandfather meant to forget about his sisters.

I think he thought about them less and less until they occupied a tiny corner of his memory. It took big events to revive those thoughts. Perhaps one was his wedding, when Dora Aiden became Dora Scruggs. He may have paused before kissing his bride, and remembered the sisters he'd barely known.

And then there was the funeral of his daughter, Ozelma.

Death was no friend to my grandfather, but it was no stranger. He may have looked at his children sitting on a wooden pew, crying over the baby in the casket and seen himself grieving. So he sighed, closed his eyes for a second, and retreated to his past.

His tears might have surprised him. He'd shed so many: over Elnora and Dora, then his mother and grandfather. All before he turned fourteen. Yet there were more, for a little girl whose life was shorter than her mother's pregnancy.

When he opened them, he was a father, not a brother; a man, not a little boy. He did what Scruggses do. He put the memories back in their places and kept quiet.

Life was doing its work anyway. He and his wife would have one more child, my father, before their divorce. My grandfather moved in with another woman and married her. He simply was not there to talk about Dora and Elnora.

He provided the model for his children. He didn't talk

about his deceased sisters, and they didn't speak of Ozelma.

Her life is a short story. She was born in September 1927. She died the following April. She was a beautiful baby, dressed with care and buried in her Easter clothes.

My father never knew Ozelma. He came a year later in March 1929.

On Easter Sunday.

Was he the answer to a prayer, the granting of his mother's plea for a second chance, with a vow to be more careful next time?

If I could, I would ask Dodo whether she stood over Daddy while he slept, listening to his deep, even breathing to calm her fears. Did she fuss over him more than she did over the others? Did she keep him by her side, while his sisters ran off to play?

Did she? Did he know why?

Only she could have told him about his sister. The other children wouldn't have been able to explain. Katherine and William were in elementary school when Ozelma died; Aunt Irene was four and Aunt Helen was three. There was no time to include her in their games and schemes. She never grew old enough to run with them, tattle on them, to hug them when they came home from school.

My father and his siblings knew Ozelma by the sadness in their mother's voice when she spoke about their little girl. They knew the baby by their mother's insistence that good clothes be worn immediately, not hoarded for a special occasion which, like Ozelma's Easter, might never arrive.

Yet I can't fault my grandparents for their reticence when I look at my relationship with my family: my sister and brother and his children. We talk about the present.

I complain about the newspaper stories I'm reporting, about obtuse bosses with no respect for my creativity and vision. My sister interrupts with stories about her principal and the children in her classes. My brother frets about his karate school in between bragging over his students' trophies and national rankings.

We are so caught up in adult concerns and goals, we rarely stop to glance over our shoulders. We mimic the generations preceding us. We don't talk about what used to be, and who was there with us.

One day, I fear, my brother's children will come across a list of their grandfather's siblings. They will look at the names and ask the same questions I asked:

Who were these people?

They will see one name in particular, Irene Elizabeth Scruggs, and realize this woman could not have been their grandmother. They will pick up the telephone—if telephones still exist—call and say, "Who was Irene Elizabeth Scruggs?"

I will echo Cousin Bertha.

"She was your grandfather's sister . . ."

I'll wait for the inevitable follow up, "Why didn't you tell us about her?"

"I don't know," I'll say. "She just never came up . . ."

Chapter Eleven

"If somebody asked you to describe Aunt 'Rene, what you say?"

My sister took a minute to think about how she would present our aunt to our nieces and nephews. Then she asked a question.

"Emotionally or physically?"

"Physically, first."

"She was a light brown person with brown eyes. She was short."

"Did she have good hair?"

"She had a perm!" My sister's voice mocked me for even asking such a question. We were Scruggses. Good hair, almost straight hair belonged to some other family, not to ours.

"What would you say about her emotionally?"

Jennifer paused longer this time, weighing the words that might survive her.

"She was a person who loved, but didn't know how to show it."

She was, then, my father's sister, showing affection in deeds, not words.

My mother and aunt were both named "Irene Elizabeth," a coincidence if there ever was one. They had both been called by their first names all their lives, so there was no recourse to a middle name. My cousins called them "Aunt Irene," even when both were in the same room. "We always knew who they were talking to," Mama said.

My brother and sister didn't even think of softening my aunt's name the way I did.

"I was scared of her," Max admitted. Awe inflated his voice, so he sounded decades younger than his forty years. My brother is a broad man, with shoulders and chest wide enough to compete against heavyweight black belts at karate tournaments. With that admission, though, he was again the skinny little boy whose knees looked like knobs on a pair of wooden sticks. "Maybe I saw her speak out somebody. I don't know. I left her alone."

"I called her Aunt Irene," my sister said. "I didn't like her. She was bossy. . . ."

My laughter interrupted her.

"I am not bossy," Jennifer said. "I am opinionated, but I'm not bossy."

I laughed again. If any of the nieces could have been Aunt 'Rene's daughter, it would have been Jennifer.

She had Aunt 'Rene's almond eyes, and round face with the weak chin that we'd gotten from the Aidens. But Aunt 'Rene didn't inherit her mother's full lips and wide nose. Aunt 'Rene's face belonged to her Daddy, as surely as my father's face mimicked his mother's.

My aunt had inherited her father's nose, with its sharp, defined bridge, as well as his light brown skin. She wasn't as pale as Cousin Bertha, but she was far lighter than her brother and sister.

Did Aunt 'Rene inherit her father's demeanor? I think so. My grandmother Dodo was pliable, not one to stomp the floor, much less raise her voice or hand in self-defense. She owned a cafe, a joint really, selling liquor and food. She watched a boyfriend simply take it from her and install his newest lady friend.

"Dodo didn't do a thing," my mother spat out. Her eyes burned while she imagined all the hell she would have raised if she had stood in Dodo's place. "She just said, 'I'll turn it over to Jesus.' "

No, my mother wouldn't have waited on the Lord, and neither would Aunt 'Rene. She would have smiled and schemed, stroking the man's face as she counted the money that would find its way into her purse. The man would be gone when she was through, discarded with leftover food and stale beer.

She would have stood her ground and defended it. She would have sounded an alarm with her favorite saying. "If you don't start no s, h, there won't be no i, t."

"Sure did," my sister laughed. "She used to say that all the time."

"She used to press our hair."

And pop us popcorn. And meticulously paint our fingernails, so that the stubby, bitten tips seemed as glamorous as she was.

"Daddy didn't want us to turn out like his sisters," I told Jennifer.

"I didn't know that! Who told you that?"

"Mama. That's why he was so hard on us, that's why he didn't let us go to parties sometimes. . . ."

He judged us with a parent's prophetic eye, or maybe fear clouded his vision. He needn't have worried. I decorated the wall at parties, waiting for violins to sound when someone cute glanced my way. He would hear the soaring strings as he made his way over to me, held out his hand and led me to the floor while the Delfonics crooned, "La, la, la, la, la . . . I love you."

I waited, watching Jennifer turn down dances until, tired of saying no, she walked sullenly to the middle of the room.

"Well, I never knew Aunt Irene to work," Jennifer noted. "What did she do?"

I saw her once on my way from school. It was far, far from our neighborhood, on the rich white part of town. I attended a special class for intellectually gifted students. After years of getting to school on our own, the district finally hired taxicabs to transport us. The rides made for a long day, since I was the first stop in the morning and one of the last stops in the afternoon. In between, the driver picked up students from another class similar to ours. Except their parents had money. And maids.

Those kids sat with their friends. I usually kept quiet while the driver traveled the broad avenues of their neighborhood. Little clusters of black women stood at selected corners. Coats covered their bodies, scarves covered their heads, hiding their identity and turning them into barely distinguishable pillars.

We'd stopped at a stop sign. While the driver looked for oncoming cars, I scrambled to the window and rapped as quickly and as hard as I could. When the women looked up, I waved and grinned. Finally, Aunt 'Rene saw me and answered with a wave and smile of her own. I could see her pointing and talking to the other women. "My niece," she said. They smiled and nodded, surprised and pleased to see a black child sharing in the privileges granted to their employers' children.

"Who is that?" The rich kids saw me for the first time. Perhaps they also realized that the women on the corner had lives and purposes apart from the big houses and the wide streets.

"That's my aunt." I sat back, satisfied, and retreated into silence until I got home.

I truly loved Aunt 'Rene, but I knew what my Daddy thought. I knew there was something slightly shady about the men in her life. She was born a Scruggs. Her only son was a Fitzpatrick, but her last name was Thomas. I knew her boyfriends seemed to slip in and away, as if they were evading other commitments and responsibilities.

Once I was brave and curious enough to raise the issue with my mother. "Aunt 'Rene's boyfriend, Buck, is he married?"

"Yes." Mama looked me straight in the eyes, waiting for the next question. But I let the matter drop. At nine or ten, I was old enough to know that married people were not supposed to have special friends. Their time and attention was supposed to be dedicated to spouses and children. I knew the rules of marriage. And I knew adults broke rules all the time. I wanted to confirm my suspicions for my own safety.

I suspected that Buck's arrivals and departures were Aunt 'Rene's business and I should watch myself. Nashville wasn't even a big small town when it came to black folks. Everyone knew everything, even if they didn't tell.

I was growing up. I could solve puzzles. I could keep secrets. I was maturing.

I could keep my side of the room neat. I could hang up my clothes, without a reminder from Aunt 'Rene.

"It takes just as much time to hang up your coat as it does to throw it on the couch." She faced us with her hands on her hips and legs spread apart, taking the stance that anthropologists claim came from a Congolese war posture. She was ready to fight, angry over repeating those instructions fifty times in twenty minutes.

And Jennifer was ready to fight, too. She sucked her teeth and rolled her eyes, dangerous gestures for a seven-year-old facing an elder. She picked up her coat and marched to the closet. "When are you going home?"

"Not today. Now hang up that coat."

I obeyed without a word, thankful for the opportunity to see the floor and the cushions of the sofa. When I finally got my own room, I promised myself, my coat would be on a hanger in the closet. I'd make up my bed every day. My books would be stacked and organized. My quarters would be as orderly as Aunt 'Rene's apartment.

She lived by herself in the projects. Her floors were clear and her furniture was ready for guests.

Her ashtrays held half-smoked cigarettes, perched precisely on the rim so the tips would remain unsoiled and ready for her to return with a match. She was an adult, free of intrusive children who disturbed the life she'd so carefully arranged. I wanted to live like that. I wanted to be able to put my books down, assured of their location when I came back hours or days later.

I'm sure Daddy saw the admiration in my eyes. I'm sure my mother told him how happy I was when I spent the night at Aunt 'Rene's. Or maybe he'd seen me sitting behind my sewing machine, intent on stitching a straight seam, and caught a glimpse of the child his sister had been. He replayed scenes from her life and his, opportunities offered and denied, snares disguised as escapes, and wanted better for me.

But I had matured enough to know what I wanted. I wanted a radio tuned to my favorite station whenever I clicked on the dial. I wanted my own space, small enough to be intimate without being confining. I wanted my family on my own terms, at my own convenience.

I wanted Aunt 'Rene's home, and that was all.

Chapter Twelve

If proximity makes a family, then I belonged to a clan. Like Cousin Bertha, I was raised with cousins from my mother's and my father's sides. We weren't family reunion kin—the folks who you only see once every two or three years. We were sleep over cousins—the kids you board with for days or weeks, until their parents get tired and send everyone to *your* house.

Every summer, Aunt Helen put up with us until she needed a break, or my mother missed her children. We shuttled back and forth from their home in south Nashville to our house in east Nashville. We spent days, nights, sometimes weeks, playing and fighting together. We were like brothers and sisters.

That kind of closeness endures.

Cousin Bertha hadn't seen my grandfather for fifty years before she met me. But she was insulted when I asked whether she'd forgotten him.

How could you forget someone who slept beside you, and ran through the yard with you? My grandfather was more than a cousin. He was a companion, a compatriot who lived in the special land of little children. He conspired on schemes that got them into and out of trouble. Of course she remembered my grandfather.

Would I forget my cousins?

When I was younger, I thought my mother and Aunt Helen played a secret game. She would have a child, and Mama would follow. Then Aunt Helen would get pregnant again. By turns they would produce children until one got tired and bowed out. Mama surrendered victory when she had my brother. Aunt Helen continued, having three more children until her two oldest walked through the door with sons and daughters of their own. Siblings, first cousins, and second cousins—our phrase for first cousins once removed—ran in and out the house, slamming doors, letting in flies, and straining the nerves of our elders. We were a whirlwind of arms and legs, punctuating our entrances and exits with screams and shouts that escaped whenever and wherever we opened our mouths.

There were other cousins on my mother's side. My great-aunts sent their sons to Nashville each summer. And my mother's youngest uncle, Johnny, had children who were only weeks younger than we. But Uncle Johnny's two sons and daughter inhabited the same amount of space as we did. Aunt Helen's crew surged past the compact territory of our family into a land as vast as a continent.

There were borders. The oldest girls, Nannie (or "Toots") and Mary Katherine, lived in a place of their own, a country we youngsters were rarely permitted to enter. We knocked before walking into their rooms. We paused before reaching for their food. The warning "That's Toots'!" signaled a retreat and reconsideration of whatever assault we'd planned to launch. The girls and their brother, Sam junior, had finished high school. They were working and raising children. They were "grown" and we left them alone.

We didn't need them anyway. We held the power of the majority.

When I became a teenager, content to read, gossip on the telephone, and daydream about adult adventures, my mother finally felt safe enough to divulge her prior vulnerability. "When it was just two of y'all everything was fine," she said. "But when three of y'all were around, that third one could always think up something to do."

She had no defenses against four, five, or sometimes seven when Aunt Helen's crew joined our trio.

We weren't impudent. Talking back or blatant disobedience would have resulted in a trial and certain death by switch. Neither she nor Daddy could watch us constantly. He didn't try. When the kids took over the house, he left. Mama had to hold down the fort all by herself. She knew she was outflanked. And so did we.

Still she maintained the front when she caught us all in a bedroom with the lights out.

"What are you all doing?" Her question quieted the chatter that must have tumbled down from the bedroom upstairs. When she opened the door, sudden light from the hallway blinded us and turned her small frame into a massive silhouette.

"Why is the door closed? Cut on the light!" She hit the switch before we could even move.

She expected shifting feet, sliding eyes and surreptitious attempts to straighten out our clothes. We met her scowl with giggles, nudging each other to stand straight so someone could finally speak.

"Well, we were trying to see . . . we wanted to know . . ."

The veneer of pre-adolescent sophistication dissolved into another round of laughter until her frown sobered us up.

". . . if we could see Kenny's teeth in the dark."

Kenny stood in the narrow aisle separating the twin beds. His lips were pulled so far apart they seemed to split his face. He was waiting, like the rest of us, for Mama to nod her head and flick off the light so we could continue our scientific experiment. We were sure our hypothesis would be verified, that Kenny's limbs would merge with the darkness. Only his teeth and the whites of his eyes would be visible, brilliantly hinting at the presence of a boy who had become one with the night.

Mama understood what we were doing. We had reduced the darkest one of us to a caricature, a living, breathing darky. And he'd stood for it.

"Y'all don't have any sense! Get out of here! Go downstairs! No, go to bed!"

Where? How did seven kids fit in bedrooms meant for three? We spread out pallets and pulled out the couch, all the while whining "What did we do? We didn't do nothing!"

"And don't try to keep the TV on till midnight," she warned.

How did the adults get a rest? We went to bed, but not to sleep. We talked and we played. We ignored the threats until exhaustion finally shut us up. The night was too short for the overwhelmed adults. They groaned when cartoons interrupted their rest at six on a Saturday morning.

We were a mass back then, flowing into our individual maturity but still belonging to the whole.

Now that we are older, routine and distance separate us. Procrastination keeps us apart in spite of protestations to stay in touch. Yet we are close; we were raised up together.

That bond has not linked succeeding generations. I know Mary Katherine's son, but not her grandchild. I see her brother

Gerry regularly. But I can count the number of times I've seen his son on one hand. I've never seen my cousin Charles's wife. When Aunt Helen dies, I will not know many of her descendants.

When we get together, we laugh and trade stories, using our memories to deny the truth. And if I cannot hold onto people I knew so intimately, could I even touch someone whose name I never heard?

Chapter Thirteen

Traveling through Williamson County felt like stepping into a soothing embrace. The highway rose and fell between soft round hills that would have indicated mountains if I'd been driving though east Tennessee or North Carolina. But I was in middle Tennessee, heading south from Nashville.

This was the route I'd taken to and from Mississippi when I wanted a respite from fields of cotton. Sometimes I drove north from Jackson along the Natchez Trace. As I rode closer to home, the ground swelled slowly but distinctly. Somehow the land opened up and I seemed to be traveling right into the horizon. The terrain spread itself before me, hills on my left and right, carving curves from the sky.

I could settle down here and nestle in a hollow. I'd be as warm as if I curled up in the arm of my couch, pulled my legs under my body and wrapped up in my quilt. I'd overlook the strip malls and the gridlock. I'd unlock my doors and open my windows wide, allowing the chatter of crickets and birds to invade my home and entice me into my day.

"Franklin got all kinds of nice homes now, all these interstates, it's all built up," Cousin Edna had told me. "It's not country like it used to be." She'd heard the longing in my voice, the yearning for a place to rest and retreat. She'd heard all the misimpressions of an occasional visitor who enjoyed freedom and mobility. Her generation had left because such opportunities were not available in Williamson County back then.

"I got tired of the country," she said.

Not that she wanted for much, she said. "There were all kinds of vegetables, fruit, hogs and cows. You could get everything you want."

Still, she repeated, "It's different now." She couldn't make me understand and she didn't try. Only the tone of her voice warned that an endless horizon didn't guarantee liberty. Darkness could exist in a bright, cloudless sky.

The old Scruggs place lay on the fertile banks of the West Harpeth River. Librarians and researchers gave me meticulous directions. I got confused as soon as I drove beyond the city limits, where the county turned into a maze of roads and turnoffs. My family claimed a place among these hills, but I lacked the nonchalant familiarity with routes and shortcuts. I pulled out my maps. I questioned cashiers at one too many gas stations. I turned around and headed toward the city, then stopped halfway and retraced my route. I watched my odometer rise while my gas gauge dropped.

The closest I got to Ed Scruggs's farm was a picture that I'd found in the county's archive. I was familiar with the place, even though I'd never seen it. All its contents were listed in the documents filed after Old Ed died.

He wasn't one of the richest men in the county. If the inventories were any indication, however, he'd lived a comfortable life and left much behind. His heirs stood to inherit "feather beds and looking glasses . . . one hundred fifty head of hogs," and dozens of negroes (with a lower case n).

But the photograph was taken in the twentieth century, not the nineteenth. It didn't show fields, or the plows that had been included in the court filing. Instead the camera had caught a group of black men sitting in front of a trench that was deep and wide enough to hold dozens of corpses. They were mining phosphate.

This was a portrait of hard work, dirty work, of sweating and bending one's back to make another man, a white man, rich. This was the truth of Williamson County, as true as the mansions and strip malls that were devouring the old farms.

Cousin Edna's voice had hinted at events too dangerous to mention. Franklin was a good place to be from, but Nashville was a better place to be.

Suddenly her voice lightened, like the sky after a summer downpour.

"We used to go back and visit. We went back to church. . . ." She spoke of ice cream socials and church suppers, of flirting and courting under her elders' watch.

She spoke of the place that had been her home, and Dick's.

Cousin Bertha had told me one story about my great-great-grandfather. He'd gotten mad at some white person and run away. He didn't go far from the plantation, though, just to a ditch in the woods. He stayed there for three weeks and then returned.

"What happened to him?" I asked.

"Nothing," she told me.

The little story challenged everything I knew and all I'd assumed about slavery. I understood that Dick's situation was so unbearable that he would want to leave. But what was so compelling about his life that he would return?

I shared my confusion with a historian friend. We both agreed that Dick had put his master on notice by showing how easily a slave could slip away.

But why stop? Why nibble at freedom? Why not swallow hard, take one's chances and run.

"I don't know," my friend said. His voice had taken on the detached inquiring tone of a scholar considering a historical puzzle. "It's easy to run away, but hard to get away."

I listened to Cousin Edna, and I began to realize the difference. Running away is a matter of leaving. Getting away is a matter of leaving things behind.

Dick was a young man in 1847 if, as the census states, he was born in 1828. His valuation of five hundred and fifty dollars meant the estate saw an asset, not a liability. Dick would enrich the family throughout the five years it took to settle his late owner's estate. He was strong, a field hand who could plant and plow, sow and reap. He'd already demonstrated his resilience simply by surviving to manhood. Eventually he would make babies—more assets for whoever owned him.

Could he have been worth even more? Historians say that men like Dick sometimes sold for more than a thousand dollars. But the inventory listed no slaves worth such high amounts. Perhaps prices in middle Tennessee and other parts of the Upper South were lower than those in the Deep South: Alabama, Mississippi, and Georgia.

Perhaps assessors did the white family a favor, and undervalued the property to save on taxes. Or maybe Dick's personality diminished his worth: perhaps he was lazy or stubborn. Maybe he would sooner steal an axe than pick it up. Maybe he challenged the overseer whenever possible. Possibly he was always on the lookout for a way to escape.

Still, if Dick were more trouble than he was worth, I'd have never found his name on the inventory. His master would have cut his losses and put Dick up for sale.

So I think that my great-great-grandfather was an average slave, caught in the inherent contradictions of being a human being who was legally defined as property. I know he had hopes and dreams; everyone does. I wonder, though, if he dreamed of freedom. It would have been a sparkling prize, not easily attainable. Too many obstacles stood in his way.

The paved thoroughfares that carried me over hills and through valleys were hard dirt roads in Dick's day. They were routes too open for an escaping slave to risk. He would have traveled over the river and through the woods, northwest to Kentucky, across the massive river into Ohio. He might have stopped in Cincinnati to catch a breath. But he wouldn't have stayed. The town was a popular destination for fugitive slave catchers. Dick could not be free from the bondage and fear until he made it to the other side of Lake Erie, into Canada. He would be hundreds of miles away from Ed Scruggs's farm then, far from the people, black and white, who claimed his body and his heart.

Laws and traditions shaped Dick's destiny, as surely as the broken laws and traditions of segregation determined mine. Legislators forged each link in the chain designed to keep him in the narrow space allotted to those like him.

I can't say "people like him" because legally he was not a person. He was collateral for a loan, or a down payment on a hundred acres of land. He was the force guiding the plow that turned the soil that guaranteed his master's prosperity. He was a necessity, like the horses that pulled the buggy, or the hoe that kept weeds from smothering the crops.

But Dick was not a person. If the legal framework of Southern society had prevailed, he would have always been a com-

modity. Acknowledging his humanity would have revealed the
immorality and deceit at the core of antebellum life. It was
easier to tighten the reins that held slaves and slaveholders to
their prescribed places. Legislators fashioned severe consequences for champing at the bit.

The price of emancipation, whether stolen by escape or
awarded through a master's largesse, was nothing less than ex-
ile.

In 1831, when Dick was only three or four years old, his world
began to come to an end. Abolitionist William Lloyd Garrison
celebrated the year by publishing the first issue of his newspaper
Liberator. That August, the shouts of Nat Turner's revolutionaries
echoed from Southampton, Virginia, south through the Caro-
linas, west to Alabama and Mississippi, and back north to Tennessee and Kentucky.

White slave owners realized the enemy worked in their
fields and raised their children. A hoe could chop off a head as
efficiently as it chopped weeds. The hand that stirred the pot
could poison the stew. The whites clamped down, drafting law
after law to curtail the minimal autonomy the slaves enjoyed.

In Tennessee, the fear of slave rebellions ebbed and flowed
for twenty years. Free blacks lived in the state, but their position
was even more precarious. In 1849, two years after Ed Scruggs
died, manumissions were allowed at the master's death, and
then only if written in the will. But freedmen were legal non-
entities. So in 1854, legislators resolved their dilemma. A freed-
man or woman would have to leave Tennessee, not for the
North or Canada, but east. To Africa. To Liberia. There was no
doubt. To be black in Tennessee was synonymous with being
enslaved.

Dick's place was working the fields of Ed Scruggs's farm. The boundaries were narrowly drawn; still his life there was vital. His mother, Eliza, lived with nine of her children. If the slaves were inventoried according to age, Dick was second oldest, between Abe and Anthony.

Nine families lived on that farm: some single parent, others with fathers and mothers raising their offspring. In the small world of the plantation, they all intermingled until a single bloodline emerged and all were kin. There was, I'm convinced, a measure of stability in Dick's life that provided some kind of comfort. He'd grown up with the routines of plantation life. He tended the crops with people who had known him since birth. He belonged to the plantation and it belonged to him.

And then Ed Scruggs's death thrust Dick and the others into another world.

A master's death caused fear and apprehension in the slave quarters. . . . Slave families were at the mercy of legatees, or heirs . . . or creditors.

—Historian John Hope Franklin

Death surprised Ed. Maybe an unexpected illness came and took his breath. He could have been out hunting, when a bullet meant for an animal pierced his heart instead. Or his end might have been more mundane. A nick from a rusty nail could have locked his jaws and pulled the water from his body until he willingly surrendered his life. I searched, but I never found how or why he died. I only know that he passed away, like the rich man in the New Testament whose storehouses meant nothing when God called for his soul.

No, Ed expected to live past his fifty years. He looked around him and saw his wife and toddling children, the acreage on river's banks and slaves enough to guarantee a harvest. He did not stop to consider this: no one knows the day nor the hour when they must account for their life in Heaven.

So he did not write a will. When he died, he went to wrangle with the Lord while the fates of all his dependents—his wife, children, and slaves—hung in the air.

This is when my ancestor's life turns into a scene from a movie.

I see a huge white house dominating a verdant yard. I hear an iron bell, tolling, tolling. I see a somber white family gathered on a veranda, facing a yard of slaves. The family wears black. The mother cries as the oldest son steps forward to address the assembled crowd. He pauses, swallowing hard and fighting back tears. I know all this because I see his face. I see his mother's shoulders raise and fall in the rhythm of her sobs.

I only see the backs of the slaves. I have no way to differentiate one from another. They merge into a blob of bodies, as they meekly and patiently wait to hear the news they already know. The scene stops before the slaves begin to sing, before sorrow lifts their voices into song, and the melody of "Steal Away" rises from the crowd.

The camera never follows the slaves into their quarters, never catches them huddling around the hearth, laughing and crying from joy and anxiety. The scene is static, simplistic and clichéd. It is a scene that is so pervasive it replaces history. I've fought against this scene ever since I read *Gone With the Wind* at fifteen.

So it hurts to admit that parts might be true. Some slaves probably grieved over Ed Scruggs. Some slaves might have held some affection for their owner.

They all witnessed and shared intimate aspects of each

other's lives: the birth of children, the taking of a spouse. The blacks and whites had a relationship that transcended the status that defined them both.

I can't admit this possibility, because I cannot imagine life without the liberties I enjoy. I can't fathom living without the freedom to walk with my head high; to banter with my white bosses; to smile if I'm pleased and frown if I'm not. I can't conceive of censoring my expressions and weighing my words because of my station.

My ancestors lived with such minute, constant oppression. It ground them down, but they learned to manipulate it. I would rather they wore the mask, that they bowed their heads in front of the master's family, while their shoulders shook from laughter, not tears.

But my demands are as oppressive as the owners'. For my ancestors were more than slaves. They were people, with a right to their emotions and responses.

I would have preferred that Dick woke up one day with his mind on freedom, that he started running and never stopped until he stood safe from the slave catchers, in Canada. But he fashioned his own way of coping with his world. Liberty might not have been as precious as family. Maybe they were his haven.

In my script, the plantation would have been a prison. Dick would have stayed in the ditch to trick the hounds sent to track him. His capture would have guaranteed a brutal beating.

My script of his life would have him stripped to the waist and tied to a pole. His screams would have alarmed the plantation. The healer would have looked over her shoulder before she slipped into the woods. When Dick lay bleeding, she would have bathed his wounds, warning him to be quiet whenever he moaned.

But Cousin Bertha hadn't mentioned that kind of punishment. Perhaps he was never whipped.

I think he suffered something worse.

When Ed Scruggs's estate was provisionally settled, his heirs inherited a share of the slaves. But the youngest children were incapable of managing such important commodities. The court appointed guardians to handle that task. Dick was seventeen. His owner was a mere boy.

Dick became an asset in the child's trust fund.

These technicalities were probably too arcane to bother my great-great-grandfather. What mattered was what happened next. The children's slaves were parceled out, rented to whomever was willing to pay for their labor. Guardians collected the fees and deposited them into the children's accounts. Each year the guardians filed a statement of earnings with the county circuit court.

This was Dick's life for the five years it took to settle Ed Scruggs's holdings. It was a dangerous time, a chaotic time. It was a sad time for a man-child, used to living with his mother and siblings.

Yes, he lived with his family. The court filings proved it. The first inventory of Ed Scruggs's estate set a pattern that was followed by all the successive documents. The slaves were listed in groups, with adults named first, then teens, then children.

But complete families weren't maintained. Only two of Eliza's children were awarded to the minor Scruggs heirs. Those two, Dick and Anthony, were rented out as laborers. In time other circumstances intervened. Eliza's name disappeared from documents after 1847. I found no clue to her fate. Events had broken and scattered Dick's family. He saw what was happening, and that is why he ran—not to get away from the plantation, but back to it.

When I first talked to Cousin Bertha, I assumed Dick headed north and west, toward Kentucky, the Ohio River, and liberty. But those are the assumptions of a free woman, who slipped away from her family at the first opportunity.

Maybe Dick wanted another kind of freedom. Maybe he longed to walk and talk with his loved ones, to hear his mother's voice and hold his siblings' hands. Maybe the right to walk unfettered was a luxury he could live without, especially if liberty meant abandoning his family.

No, I don't think Dick plotted his journey by the North Star. I think he walked along the West Harpeth River, following its flow until it took him home.

Chapter Fourteen

I couldn't find a comb. I was there in New England, far, so far from my family and Nashville and the world I'd made as a college student in Chicago. Both were home to me.

My feet knew my neighborhood streets by heart. They carried me from my starting points to my destinations, while my mind considered the books I should have read and the exams I'd have to take. And whenever I went to Nashville, I strolled past the houses of my friends as easily as I'd done in high school.

In both places, I knew where I was, and how to get what I needed, without much consideration. That's what a home is.

Yet I was in Vermont, just hours away from Canada, where the Green Mountains met Lake Champlain. I'd gone to Middlebury College to study Russian for a summer. I thought I'd come prepared. I'd packed everything I needed: books, dictionaries, sweaters against the chill that never lifted. I'd brought hair grease and a brush. How had I forgotten a comb?

At Mama's I could have simply walked in the bathroom upstairs and rummaged in the linen closet. I'd have moved aside the shampoo and the pressing oil, reached back behind the hot irons, and pulled out an Afro comb or two.

At college I'd have groaned, counted my change, and headed to the drug store. I would have stood in front of the rack, the minutes accumulating as I decided whether I wanted a hard rubber shampoo comb or another Afro pick with a handle in the shape of a fist.

Back home, either one of them, the problem would have been solved easily. But I was in a land of strangers, where the remnants of my Southern accent grated on my own ears.

The college bookstore had combs. But they were small and pliable, with narrow teeth that couldn't penetrate my thick kinks. These were combs for white people, not blacks.

Black students went to the college; I'd met some that summer. But they didn't rely on the bookstore. They pooled their money, wrote a shopping list, and sent somebody to Albany, New York, five hours away.

I'd wanted to come here. I needed to immerse myself in Russian just to make decent grades my last year in college. My parents had shrugged and let me go, as long as I found a way to pay tuition. And I'd done it, stitching loans, grants, and work-study, catching a ride that dropped me off in front of the dorm late one New England night.

I'd closed my eyes to the white students hurrying from the dorms to the cafeteria and back to the library. I'd politely corrected whites from other language schools who mistook me for one of the other black women on campus. I thought I could handle being the fly in the buttermilk.

Until I couldn't find a comb.

I called home crying. "There are no black people here."

"What did you expect?" At least Mama didn't add, "I told you so." She was developing a modicum of tact. "You know the farther north you go, the fewer of us you find. And when you get to Maine, there aren't any of us there at all."

She ended the geography lesson by handing the telephone to Daddy.

"What's the matter?" he asked, but he already knew the answer. He'd been on a ship in the middle of the ocean, working with a dozen men he saw day in and out. He'd been the only one who had marred the color scheme.

Mama was a fighter, true. She would kick down the door and stand, hands on hips, in the threshold. Daddy's weapon was his presence, and he bore the battle scars. So he listened while I talked and cried. He knew firsthand that isolation and loneliness were the price of progress and freedom.

"You're gonna go a lot of places where there won't be any black people. . . ."

In their way, my grandmother and mother had tried to postpone that lesson. They had begged me to stay home, follow their lead, and go to Tennessee State University. I'd applied to the University of Tennessee, which was almost exclusively white. But most importantly, UT was in Knoxville, three hours from Nashville. I'd had other choices and I'd made them. We all knew where my decisions had taken me.

In reality, I'd left Nashville well before I'd applied for college. I was on my way out as a child.

My family moved back South in the sixties, when blacks decided that virtual slavery was as bad as the real thing. It had taken a war and a presidential proclamation for Dick Scruggs to be freed. Three generations later, blacks risked beatings and death to claim rights that their foreparents should have enjoyed.

Nashville in the fifties and early sixties was a "progressive" Southern city. Its racial laws weren't as restrictive as in Birmingham, Alabama, or Jackson, Mississippi. Still, segregation held sway. My siblings and I discovered it in a shoe store, of all places.

The store was our favorite stop because of a large, red, papier-mâché goose. When you pulled the goose's neck, it laid a golden, plastic egg, filled with candy and trinkets. This time, though, we ignored the goose in favor of a water fountain across the room.

Who discovered it first? Me, perhaps, because I could read "like a champ," my mother bragged. Or maybe Jennifer had deciphered the words. She was in kindergarten but she knew her letters and sounds. One of us saw the sign on the fountain and sounded it out.

C–O–L–O–R–E–D W–A–T–E–R.

One of us announced the discovery to the other two, and fantasies of blue and red water took over. When Mama came to see why we'd suddenly gotten so quiet, she found us clustered around the fountain, pushing and pushing the button until the water made a puddle at our feet.

Something was wrong, we told her. The sign said colored water, but the water is as clear as any other. "Why does it say colored water," we asked, "when this is just regular water?"

Mama turned to look at the white salesman. "You tell them," her expression said. "You explain the system you worked so hard to establish. I'm not coming to your rescue."

She always finishes the story the same way. "The white people looked so stupid."

Time rearranges incidents into a straight line, erasing details until nothing remains but a direct path from one event to the next. I remember so much about that store: choosing between black and red patent leather shoes; playing with the goose and laughing when the egg rolled into my hand.

But I don't remember "Colored Water." I don't remember discovering segregation at all. I remember watching it die.

My immediate family didn't march, or sit-in at the drugstore. Still, we did our part. One day my mother sat us down. We wouldn't be going to the shoe store for Easter shoes. We wouldn't be going downtown at all. This year, my brother would do without a new tie. My sister and I would have to wear "good" shoes from the year before. We'd wear our regular Sunday clothes, or maybe we'd get outfits from the thrift store.

She explained that Negroes had agreed to boycott downtown until we could eat wherever we wanted, and drink from any fountain in the store. We wouldn't do like some families, and head to stores in other Tennessee towns. We wouldn't be supporting segregation anywhere.

We would wear our clothes and wait. We'd get new outfits later. After the boycott ended.

When we were free.

As I listened, I knew something important was happening. Something historical was going on (although that wasn't a word I would have used at that time), and it would make a difference in my life.

Society was standing on the cusp of a new day, and I was blessed to see the transition from the old to the new. As young as I was, I understood that segregation was fading away. Integration was a promise, but whether that promise would be fulfilled was still questionable.

Still, society was being forced to acknowledge my gifts and abilities. I would have more opportunities than my parents. And more would be expected of me.

I needed to be vigilant because I would be telling these stories someday. No one could hold me back. I belonged to a vanguard generation. And I was smart enough to understand what that meant.

I was a certified genius. I was more than a quick learner. I was a seven-year-old sitting in the third grade, a tiny child who was shorter than her classmates. Yet I possessed more brainpower than the best of them.

My IQ was 137.

My second-grade teacher had complained about me almost from the beginning of the school year. "She's working the hell out of me," the woman told her husband.

I wasn't bad—yet.

I loved my teacher, Mrs. Claiborne. She was short and pretty, like my mother. She was light-skinned, fair enough that my younger brother mistook her for white when he became her student four years later. He cried when we told him that, despite her straightened hair and freckles, Mrs. Claiborne certainly was black.

She taught all three of us, which meant that my siblings risked being compared to me, if not held up to the standard I'd set.

But I was special.

I devoured whatever Mrs. Claiborne gave me. Then I wriggled in my seat, starving for more math problems or another reading assignment. Lots of times, I turned the pages of the encyclopedia; my teacher just couldn't keep up with me. She knew she had to do something before boredom set in and my curiosity turned to mischief.

"Skip her," her husband said. Dr. Claiborne headed the psychology department at Tennessee State University. Both he and his wife knew that skipping a child was an extraordinary move.

An intellectually gifted child wasn't always socially or physically on par with the older children in the higher grade. And those children sometimes resented the younger, smarter child. Would they take their feelings out on me at recess? Would they ignore me in the lunchroom?

But Mrs. Claiborne considered the alternative: a creative student with too much time on her hands and an audience of twenty peers. She arranged a conference with my mother and grandmother, the teachers who knew me best.

I could tell Mama had something on her mind when she talked to me in a private place. We were alone. My sister and brother were nowhere around, nor were my grandmother or my great-grandmother.

"Stephanie, how would you like to be in the third grade?"

"When?" School had already started, but I hadn't even gotten my first report card. How could I pass to a higher grade when I hadn't finished the one I was in?

"Soon."

"Would I have a new teacher?"

"Yes, Mrs. Lee."

She was all right, but she wasn't Mrs. Claiborne. Mrs. Lee was taller and heavier, like my grandmother. In fact, my grandmother taught at my school. Why couldn't I go to her class?

"Because you're her granddaughter," Mama said.

That explanation didn't make sense to me. My grandmother told me what to do at home. Why couldn't she tell me what to do at school? If I had to leave Mrs. Claiborne, I wanted to go to my grandmother's class. No, I didn't want to go to Mrs. Lee's room, and no, I didn't want to go to the third grade.

"Well, you're going," Mama said. That was progressive parenting in the early sixties: present the child with a fait accompli disguised as her personal choice. I wasn't happy, but I didn't argue. The next day, Mrs. Lee introduced me to her class.

Later that year, I remember being called from my room to meet with a young white lady. She closed the door and we talked. Rather, I talked while she placed funny cards and blocks of various shapes on the table.

I told her about my favorite book, the one I'd just finished. It was called *How Big is Big?*

"Do you know that the largest number in the world, beside infinity, is a googolplex?" I asked. "And that atoms are made of neutrons, protons, and electrons?" I didn't know anything about subatomic theory, then.

I was only seven.

I was meeting with her because I'd talked to another psychologist who supervised the city's Negro schools. He didn't say anything after our conversation. Instead he scheduled a meeting with the lady who handed out the blocks and watched me arrange them. She handed me a pencil and I circled answers on a piece of paper.

The next year, I wasn't in Mrs. Lee's room. I'd left to go to a new school.

What is the world of a child but school and church, family and friends? At seven going on eight, I'd become an explorer. My test scores were so high, I was admitted to a "special class" for gifted and talented students.

There were eighteen of us: six girls and twelve boys; fifteen whites and three blacks. We were geniuses, precious resources worthy of the best the district had to offer. Other pupils studied addition and long division. We learned set theory and simplified algebra. My friends learned to spell. We studied English and French.

My friends walked to school in twos and threes. Each morning I stood at the bus stop by myself. I rode downtown, where I waited to transfer to another bus. Thirty minutes later, I got off at my school, on the other side of town. The commute took an hour, one way.

The kids in my neighborhood walked along familiar streets. They knew the houses by the children who ran out to greet them each morning. I didn't see my classmates until I got downtown. We'd board the bus and head to the seats in the back. Our goal was to sit on the same side of the aisle, so we could talk and play on our way to school.

We practiced our own brand of segregation: boys with boys and girls with girls. Lisa and I sat on one seat. Mike and Steve shared another. But Lisa left me when we got to school. She played with the other girls, the white girls.

My best friend was Susan Kaminitz. She was the only Jewish girl in the class.

I was an outsider at home as well. I spoke with the rhythms and phrasing of the white children who surrounded me all day. I didn't have the relaxed, sensual pronunciation of children on my block. My vowels were distinct. When I said "the," you could hear the "th."

My neighbors looked up to me. I never looked down on them, but around and outside the streets where I lived. I measured my neighborhood with the worldly eyes of a person who'd seen bigger and better. I knew places where the yards were larger than our houses. I loved where I lived, but I knew there was more to Nashville than my friends could imagine.

My mother had jumped at the opportunity to get me in this class. She wanted me to be free to discover my strengths and abilities, to soar as far as my intelligence would take me. But along with the languages and the math, I learned another lesson.

Climbing up to success meant climbing away from friends and family. It was perfectly acceptable to leave them behind in order to reach your potential—as long as you didn't forget where you'd come from.

I could acknowledge my roots from anywhere, and I did for years—until my father's death showed me I couldn't count on my loved ones standing where I left them until I was ready to return.

PART THREE

Chapter Fifteen

The piano bench was so old and hard that squirming brought me little comfort. I was really sleepy, but it wouldn't do to doze in front of the entire congregation. I was the minister of music. I needed to be alert to the dynamics of service: the soft melodies that filled the silence as the minister came to the pulpit; the driving chords and runs when the Spirit took over and she delivered its message instead of the one she'd planned.

Instead I was on the verge of closing my eyes and nodding my head.

I shook myself and leaned into the keyboard to improvise a song on the softest, highest notes of the piano. The assistant pastor was preaching today. I played a little something while she observed the protocol of an apprentice. She greeted the church elders in the name of the Lord. Then she thanked the presiding minister, who had graciously stepped aside and allowed a student to take her place. After a few more words to relax the congregation, she eased into her message.

"I had this dream about my aunt . . . and she came to give me a street number . . ."

I laughed with the rest of the church. Some of us were poor, some of us less so, but we all knew about numbers. They were the tickets to our dreams, and those of our parents and grandparents. Generations of hopes and fantasies were distilled into three digits written on a piece of paper and secured with a quarter, or even a dollar if the gambler was feeling flush and lucky. We boxed them, hedging the bets on all the possible combinations, while we prayed for the windfall, which always seemed just a day away.

We could have saved the money. And many of us did, sensibly depositing the daily dollar into a bank account instead of turning it over to the numbers man. But a visitation from a dead relative often convinced the most sober person to try his or her luck. A sign from an ancestor wouldn't be ignored.

"I went all over town, trying to play this number . . ." She didn't reveal it. More than a couple of us would have bet on it ourselves if she had. She was in training to lead a flock to salvation, not destruction. No use tempting the weak as well as the strong.

"But God's hand was in the plan . . ." The number fell straight, just like the auntie had promised. The minister missed hundreds of dollars, though, because God had obstructed her efforts. The money would have been a curse, not a blessing, a distraction from the path God had set for her.

"When your relatives come in dreams, it's really Satan working to tempt you . . ."

I struck up a hymn that was bound to bring the unbelievers to their feet and perhaps down to the altar and through the opened "doors of the church."

After service, I would head the other way, away from the congregation and away from a traditional black church for good.

I'd reached a fork in my road. I could no longer sit comfortably in the pews. I'd felt my ancestors, talked with them. I had taken my problems to them, and they had answered me. They were real to me now, real in my heart, and their touch had reached deep in my soul.

The Kenyan theologian John Mbiti looked at the continent of Africa. He tallied the languages, cultures, and cosmologies of hundreds of ethnic groups, and found a belief common to them all: the confidence in the existence of their ancestors.

Mbiti said the ancestors are not spirits in the Western way: shapeless, barely communicative, floating ectoplasm. African ancestors are merely one step removed from the world of the living. They walk with us and talk to us. They eat with us, abiding on the margins of our lives until their names finally drop from the lips of their descendants. By then they've retreated to another realm, which Mbiti named Zamani.

Zamani is the past of myth, a temporal region undiscovered by Americans who equate mythology with fiction. In Zamani, time melts into the cosmos, creating the place we call eternity. The transition to Zamani takes about five generations. Until then, they linger even though their flesh and bones have joined with the soil of their grave. They are in no hurry to leave, unless their descendants push them away.

A person without any relatives, or no attendants willing to keep his or her memory alive, is doomed to become a spiritual nonentity. They wander in a kind of purgatory, I think, crying for release and recognition. When I called the names of my foreparents—Dick and Julia; William the father and the son; Dora and Elnora—I revived their spirits as surely as if I'd breathed over dying embers and ignited the flames.

I'm not so vain as to think my foreparents had been completely forgotten. Maybe Cousin Bertha passed down names and even pictures to her children and their progeny. Maybe other cousins, lost to me, had called their names.

But Dick and the others were unknown to the circle of my family. Aunt Helen had never heard of her father's twin sisters, much less the man who sheltered them all. My mother talked about her in-laws as if she'd been raised in their home. Still, the early generations of Scruggses were news to her, too.

I'd stumbled upon my family by carefully and tediously reading entry after entry of microfilm. I'd gone looking for one and found them all. They must have been waiting.

They had been waiting.

Chapter Sixteen

The rain had stopped, but the sky hadn't cleared. Fog hung right above the ground, as if the clouds had fallen to earth and, conquered by gravity, were unable to return to the sky. Yet the day wasn't dank. When I stepped from the car, the air enfolded me, like a warm, fuzzy blanket.

I'd driven out to an old plantation that had sat on the outskirts of Richmond until highways and sprawl brought the city to the country. The house wore its history well. Violets and pansies covered the lawn and tinted the air so that the mansion seemed shrouded in purple and lilac. Their scent had oozed into the droplets of fog. I breathed deeply, bringing spring itself into my lungs.

I'd come to the house to pick up a press kit for a garden tour. The publicity noted the mansion belonged to Louis Ginter, a tobacco magnate. Before Ginter, tobacco was sold in pouches. The smoker took a few loose leaves, arranged them on smoking paper, and rolled a cigarette. Ginter mechanized the process, producing uniformly rolled cigarettes by the hundreds of thousands, if not millions. He made as much money as his machine-made cigarettes—and created an industry. He looked for a way to spend and flaunt his new money, and found the mansion I now glimpsed through the rearview mirror of my car.

I headed into downtown Richmond, stopping for a cup of coffee before parking in front of the art gallery where I worked. I anticipated a quiet Monday. We were closed on Mondays, but folks rarely stopped by even when we were open. All our grant applications had been submitted, and our next opening wouldn't be held for several weeks.

I sipped my coffee, appreciating the solitude. I was surrounded by beauty, constantly reminded that I had finally earned a place among creative people, and the right to express my gifts.

I was exploring photography and quilting. One flowed into the other when I found myself cutting my pictures into strips and arranging them as if they were pieces of my latest quilt top. Still I was a writer, first and foremost. When left to myself, I didn't reach for a camera or a needle and thread; I picked up my journal and pen.

I hadn't counted on this revelation when I left Charlottesville and academia to move to Richmond.

I was, according to my mother, on the verge of success. I'd arrived at the University of Virginia with a doctorate from an Ivy League institution. I was teaching in a field that blacks had rarely broached. The entire year, though, I'd brushed away a growing certainty that a life of scholarship wasn't what I needed.

I was hungry to interact with the world beyond the intimate campus of Thomas Jefferson's educational monument, to offer my talents to others besides students bent on medical and law schools. I wanted to leave behind more than mere ideas. I wanted to make art and music. When my year ended, I packed my books and left, exhilarated and frightened by my new decision.

"Here I am," I said softly, swallowing another mouthful of coffee.

It had taken four years from the time I'd left academia in 1983: four years of writing press releases, speeches, and anything else I could scrape up. Four years of working in offices, crossing my fingers that my rent check wouldn't wipe out my checking account. Four years of wondering why I'd started over, and finding meager solace in the answer.

Slowly, though, the balance began to tip in my favor. The freelance jobs accumulated. The money trickled in, then flowed more steadily. My reliance on the temporary jobs decreased as my confidence and portfolio grew. Finally I sat in the art gallery, sighing over the struggle and praising God for my growth.

I reached for the packet lying on the desk. No writer hurries to confront a blank sheet of paper, but it was time to stop procrastinating. I had to read the material and come up with some kind of an article on the garden tour.

The press release revived the image of the mansion, still stately after so many decades. I savored the last bit of my coffee as I flipped through the pages.

The property was an antebellum plantation. It had originally belonged to Thomas Prosser, who had ridden through a driving rain to "put down a slave rebellion" back in 1800.

In the seconds it took me to read that sentence, the ancestors had come and gone.

I didn't see them, or maybe I saw them so quickly I doubted the vision. I know I felt their power, their presence, and mostly their emotions.

"Ohhh," I answered. I was the only person in the gallery, yet I wasn't alone and I knew it. Or maybe I hadn't been alone and I knew that. They hadn't come to stay, just to touch me the way my mother grabbed my hand when I, expecting punishment, struggled to pull away. Theirs was not a benign embrace.

They were angry with me. They were angry with us.

"Ohhh," I repeated, ashamed. I'd been judged guilty, and my sincerity was no defense. I'd neglected my ancestors, even as I worked so hard to find them. I had seen them, but I hadn't recognized them. I remained ignorant, even while I was studying my heritage.

And they were furious.

The discovery of the slave rebellion, mentioned so casually in the press release, had rocked the city in its day. A free black man, Gabriel, conceived and organized the entire effort. He had no surname, so history gave him Prosser, the white man's name. That unwitting tribute elevated Gabriel from an item on a ledger into a person of note. It was a salute to his power and his ability to inspire respect and fear.

The white folks were afraid of Gabriel. When they captured and jailed him, James Monroe conducted his interrogation.

Monroe wanted to know more than the details of Prosser's unsuccessful revolt. He wanted to see the black man who planned an insurrection that aimed to inspire rebellion up and down the Eastern seaboard. Monroe wanted to see the black man who, he acknowledged, "possessed an intelligence far above his station in life." He wanted to see the man whose plot, though failed, revealed that the notion of black inferiority was a comfortable and ultimately dangerous lie.

White slave owners wouldn't accept the complete truth. But they were terrified enough to understand that their contented chattel were more than capable of killing their masters.

They were willing to do so.

When I'd thought about Mbiti's living dead, I'd imagined angels dedicated to my welfare and spiritual development. Some way my achievement would contribute to their spiritual elevation. It never occurred to me that my ancestors would demand more from me than recognition and a vague sense of good will. I never thought I had responsibilities to fulfill.

Were the spirits who chastised me members of Prosser's army? Had they followed me from the old plantation down to the gallery in Richmond's Shockoe Bottom? Spirits already lived in the blocks close to the James River. The gallery wasn't a short walk away from Shockoe Slip, Richmond's old commercial center. Merchants bought and sold all sorts of goods there, including slaves. My ancestors had marched up and down the streets I walked each day.

My unconsciousness enraged them.

"We are here!" They didn't speak directly to me—that would come later—but I heard them. Their declaration stayed with me for weeks, echoing whenever they felt me forgetting what they'd taught me.

"We are here," they shouted as I walked the brick streets of a gentrified historic district. "We are here," they whispered when I looked at the wrought iron gates decorating the renovated houses.

History is inescapable in Richmond, so there was no way to run from my ancestors' voices. "We are here!" "We are here!"

Finally, I could reply. "Yes, you are."

I spoke to an audience larger than the generations of spirits whose blood ran through my veins. I was talking to others, people who had given birth to descendants with closed hearts, minds, and ears. These spirits had survived slavery, only to languish in the netherworld that their descendants created by ignoring our past.

Who called the names of these spirits? Who had passed down memories of their existences?

"We are here!" they screamed, desperate to escape their fate.

"Yes you are," I answered, hoping to give them peace. "I feel you, I hear you, and I am listening."

Chapter Seventeen

I adjusted the pillow under my head and stretched my legs. This meditation stuff was not meant for anyone with a real booty, I told myself as I tried to lower the small of my back into the floor. In my effort to be perfect, to do everything correctly, I'd tightened all the muscles in my body.

"The goal is relaxation," I reminded myself. As if in response, the meditation leader dimmed the lights. I closed my eyes and followed her instructions.

"Relax your toes . . . the soles of your feet. Let all worries drain from your body . . .

"Let peace flow through you."

I'd been coming to this church for more than a year, but I still couldn't square its services and practices with those I'd known from youth. This church was a branch of the Unity School of Christianity, the folks that my family called Silent Unity. The school was famous for its twenty-four-hour prayer line.

"If you ever need to get help in a hurry," my mother had counseled, "call Silent Unity." They had a hotline to God and knew how to get a prayer through.

No one in this church would have used that phrase. Instead, they talked about "connecting with the Divine Mind," and "recognizing the in-dwelling Christ."

"Let peace flow to your arms, down through your fingers," the meditation leader directed us. "Feel each finger relax, relax every joint."

I tried to quiet the thoughts running through my mind. I'd learned not to get too anxious when my mind wandered. Instead, I blessed myself and returned to the task at hand. Still, I couldn't help wondering how I'd ended up lying on this floor instead of sitting in a pew, why I was slowly easing myself into a trance instead of moaning in prayer. Unity was so far from the Baptist Church that I asked myself if I'd taken the wrong turn on my spiritual journey.

The answer appeared in simple coincidences. My love affair with Robert had gone terribly wrong. I cried myself to sleep at night, and cried when I woke up each morning.

I didn't want to leave the bed, and that frightened me. I made myself go to work. I made myself go to church. It took all my strength to put on a dress and stockings, to clip the earrings in my ears and comb my hair.

I saw the sign on the white house across the street from my apartment complex. A casual church building meant casual dress. I picked out a clean sweater and some jeans, slipped on my shoes, and went on over.

The church really was a house, complete with a coffeemaker in the kitchen. Congregants sat at the big table and sipped coffee. Speakers from the main room brought the service to them. I stared at them for a minute. I'd never seen such informality in a house of God.

"What kind of church is this?" I wondered.

It was a mind-opening church, if nothing else. The store

sold books on astrology and reincarnation. The church encouraged acceptance of a spiritual realm where guardian angels watched over us. People chatted about signs and messages in one breath and quoted scripture in the next.

Nothing about this congregation fulfilled my assumptions about worship, or holiness, or even Christianity. But this was the church I needed. Part of me had connected with something beyond the natural world. I wasn't ready to call it the supernatural. That word conjured up Bela Lugosi's Dracula and Boris Karloff's Frankenstein.

I couldn't deny what was happening to me. When people told me their dreams, an interpretation flew out of my mouth. Little events gave me hints to future circumstances. I became convinced that the old spiritual was correct. Angels watched over me all night and all day.

The communication was always one way. They spoke and I answered. They commanded and I obeyed. I never thought to quiet myself, to sit down and ask them to enter into my presence.

Baptists didn't act that way.

My church shrugged its shoulders at 1 Corinthians 12, with its talk of speaking in tongues, and the gifts of the spirits. Those manifestations happened in the olden days, when Christ walked around like a natural man. We dwelled on 1 Corinthians 13, and the importance of love. Love was the virtue to strive for, more than faith, better than hope. Get love and everything else would follow, and if they didn't, what would it matter? Talking in tongues was gibberish without an interpreter. Paul said so himself. Love was available to any and all.

The Sanctified folks spoke of spirits with awe and fear. Spirits were Satan's agents, ready to attack or seduce the Christian into leaving God. The best defense, they claimed, was the full armor of the Lord: pray and stay faithful; remain strong in the Word; study the Bible to the exclusion of all else. Don't even think about the spirit world. Don't even read a book with spirit in the title, unless the author was a certified Christian.

But I was open to danger. I wanted to reach past all I'd been taught, to read about other paths. Still, I hadn't planned to veer from the road I'd walked since childhood.

The ancestors had other plans. When I walked into the small white house, I crossed a spiritual threshold. I'd be directed to another path, one that sometimes converged with my religious upbringing and other times diverged sharply. I'd hear the old songs with deeper understanding. I'd look at the rituals with deeper insights. I'd commune with my ancestors and guardian spirits while others were communing with God.

I'd be connected to the black church, but not always a part of it.

Chapter Eighteen

The dreams came first.

They weren't deep, mysterious sagas, but vignettes scattered throughout a nightly narrative. I always wrote down what I remembered, *when* I remembered to write down what I'd dreamed. Sometimes I managed to get out a paragraph before the entire scene evaporated. Most times I scribbled a line or two, frustrated at my inability to capture more than the skimpy summary I'd cobbled together.

But I wrote every day. Every week I reviewed my notes, looking for clues hidden there. I was headed somewhere. Heaven knew where I was going. I just saw the road, never the destination.

Whenever I got frustrated, I pulled out the little prayer card I'd bought at church. "No other way . . ." the poem read. God knows everything. The twists and turns that seem to lead away from our destiny suddenly deposit us at opportunity's door.

"No other way," I told myself when I sat before a computer keyboard, entering name after name from the pile of cards on my desk.

"No other way," I recited when the rent left no money for the gas bill.

I'd given up so much. I'd hidden my degree in a keepsake box. I didn't want it sitting on a shelf mocking me. I should have been hip deep in books and papers, working on the manuscript that would help me get tenure and security for life.

Instead I was dressing for a temporary office job at an insurance agency.

No other way. Somehow, all this tedium would release the creative energy I'd repressed. Eventually my talent would pay the rent and fill the refrigerator.

And somehow, some way, it did.

I recited the poem as I unpacked boxes. I'd found a job and an apartment. I was in the suburbs of Washington, working at a semi-weekly newspaper, but a reporter all the same. The gallery was a memory. The temporary jobs had been sustenance. Now I had a new job in a new place. I had a new life. All the work and sacrifice had paid off.

"Now I lay me down to sleep . . ." I was a grown woman, but the prayer from my childhood put to me to sleep each night. Before I closed my eyes for good, I checked the floor. The journal and pen were right there, next to the bed. I fell asleep, confident that my dreams would tell me whatever I needed to know. Still, I was puzzled when I wrote in the journal the next morning.

I dreamed about cowries, hundreds of thousands of the tiny white shells. They'd been embedded in a cliff near the sea. The soil should have been beige, like sand. Instead it was red, like the clay I'd see two years later when I drove through eastern Mississippi. Good dirt, the folks called it, so full of iron and minerals growing children ate a teaspoon as a daily tonic.

In my dream, I ignored the dirt to collect the shells. I plucked as many as I could from the cliff, then wiped them clean. I took the dream to mean a blessing was on the way; cowries traditionally doubled as money.

The windfall didn't come, but I saw cowries for the rest of the month. Cowries decorated silver bracelets and leather belts. They swung from the braids that the Afrocentric sisters wore. I decided that someone, or something, was trying to get my attention.

"The next time I see cowries, I'll ask what they mean," I decided.

The singers were the center of attention, not due to the beauty of their voices, but because of their instruments. The teenagers and I fingered the gourds, then held them cautiously. One, two, three, four, back and forth until the beaded netting surrounding the calabashes chattered rhythmically. We were playing shekeres, traditional instruments from Nigeria. I'd wanted to bring a bit of Africa, a bit of culture into this middle-class Methodist church, to challenge the teenagers in my choir with something besides the latest gospel hymn or the fastest praise song.

The instruments enchanted the teens so much, they didn't fool around like they did when *I* ran the rehearsals. Their eyes never left the singers. Everything the women did, the kids followed.

The singers had my attention, too. But I wasn't looking at their shekeres. One of the women had on cowry shell earrings. I could barely wait for the workshop to end, but politeness demanded I let the kids talk to the women first. When my turn came, I was as blunt as any teenager.

"What do those mean?" I pointed at the shells dangling from her earlobes. "I've been dreaming about cowries for a couple of weeks. It's got to be a sign."

The women looked at each other and smiled, as if they shared a secret. The one without the earrings turned and held my gaze. "They belong to an Orisha, a Nigerian deity. It's something you might want to look into."

I frowned before I realized my forehead had creased. We were in church, and they were suggesting I look into another religion, one with other deities? I wasn't sure how I felt about saints; they seemed vaguely sacrilegious to me, a Protestant. I wasn't close-minded, but I was careful.

The singer leaned over and rubbed my head as if I were a child. "Don't worry, we're not about to shave your head yet, my sister."

She wrote down a name and number while I tried to figure out what she was talking about.

"Call this sister and tell her I gave you the number. She's just been initiated and she can talk to you." Then the singer leaned over and rubbed my head again.

Both women chuckled as they left.

I made the call as soon as I got home. The woman lived in Oakland and her evening was just starting. She was all I'd been told: helpful, warm, and humble.

"Wait a minute," she said. Then another click, and suddenly I was talking to two women. She'd called her spiritual elder. I repeated my story: the dream of cowries in the cliff; the bangles with shells on the end; the way the cowries came into the church, as if they'd been sent to see me.

"You're being called by Yemaya," the elder said. The deity owned the sea, but she was more. She was as essential to life as water is to survival. She birthed the world when she receded and left land in her wake.

Nigerian slaves brought Yemaya to the New World. She was the mother of creation, just like Mary was the mother of God. . . .

"How can that be?" I interrupted. "How could I be called to follow an African god?

"I'm a Christian!"

Something had gotten a hold of me, something soft and firm. The touch was sure and strong, but gentle and comforting. Perhaps I felt the hand of the Holy Ghost. I turned to my mother and told her.

"I want to be baptized."

I was five.

I'd endured a long, hot service in my grandmother's church. No one had air conditioning in the early sixties; the ceiling fans merely circulated the hot, sticky air. I was sitting slumped against my mother on one side. My sister had capitulated to the humidity, and fallen asleep with her head in Mama's lap. But something reached inside my torpor and stirred my soul. It spoke to me and I answered.

Back then, Baptists didn't like to bring children younger than twelve to the water. The elders doubted a young child's ability to recognize the call of God. A convert needed an understanding of the responsibilities you were accepting, the commitment you were making, and a maturity that young children lack.

But the deacons didn't turn me away. When Mama explained we were leaving town that week, they got themselves together. The deaconesses scurried through the church, pulling out drawers and rummaging through closets. They came up with a long shirt and a large towel. The size wasn't important, but the color was crucial.

Candidates for baptism always wore white.

I stepped in the pool first, a little child leading the others. The preacher put one hand on my back to steady me. He raised his other hand over my head.

"I baptize you in the name of the Father, and of the Son, and of the Holy Ghost," he cried, and plunged me into the pool before I could close my eyes and my mouth. Then he pulled me up and handed me over to the deacon.

I was a Christian, a snorting, coughing new creature in Christ.

I sat quietly during the ride home. The adults talked, but their conversation passed over my head and I didn't absorb a single word. I played with my hands, waiting for them to look new, the way the hymns had promised. I wondered if my voice would be different when I finally opened my mouth, if my talk and my walk would signal my transformation.

I was only five, but I knew I'd been changed. I couldn't act as unconsciously as I had before. Decisions would have to be weighed, words would have to be watched. I had a standard to uphold. I had to treat everybody right.

I was a Christian. I'd pledged to be as much like Jesus as I could. If that meant sharing my toys, I was ready to try. If it meant going to bed without a quarrel, I'd try that, too.

I was a Christian, and even though I wasn't sure exactly how to act, I knew something had happened to me. I sat in the car and promised Jesus that I would be true for the rest of my life.

And when the revelations came, years later, I vowed not to

break my pledge. I didn't want to release my faith, just to stretch so it could contain all I was experiencing.

I set up my first altar by a book, proceeding exactly as instructed. I turned a small crate upside down and covered the surface with a white handkerchief. It would protect and purify my altar by deflecting negative energies instead of absorbing them.

I sat a powder blue ceramic saucer in the center, and placed a blue votive candle on top of the plate. Blue belonged to Yemaya, the deity who owned the cowries that had invaded my life. She liked watermelons, so I placed a tiny wooden fruit near her plate. Seven shiny dimes circled the plate; seven was her number. Just one last thing remained. I took a delicate wine glass and filled it with scented water. That took the place of the incense I was a little too cautious to burn.

I leaned back on my knees when I was done. This was my sacred space, a refuge from mundane cares and doubts. I had dedicated a corner of my room, and thus my life, to the spirits that were calling me. This was their place and mine. I lit the candle and bowed my head to pray.

To whom?

In Unity, I'd learned to invoke the Spirit within. But that Spirit was just another name for God. Would God answer if I called him Obatala, the Nigerian owner of the white cloth, instead of Jehovah? Could I talk to Obatala/God at an altar constructed for Yemaya?

Was God a woman at all?

My knees ached, so I sat down. I wasn't used to altars or candles. We Baptists prayed from the heart, unself-consciously staking our turf for Jesus. We didn't need a particular time or place. We sat or stood, raised our Bible—if we had one with us—and spoke straight to the Lord. Intentions were more important than form or fashion. After all, we were assured and warned, God knows the heart.

Who would judge me now? What spirit or spirits would peer into my soul to discern the longings I couldn't verbalize? Whose name should I call?

I looked at the altar for Yemaya and prayed the only way I knew.

"I come to you in Jesus' name . . ."

I could feel my ancestors walking with me, even though they hadn't spoken to me. I knew I was a link in an eternal chain, an infinite lineage that transcended me even as it encircled me. How many people had been brought together, through chance and circumstance, to create the children whose descendants eventually created me? I did not need to have my own offspring if I touched the lives of youngsters in my family. I wasn't only living for my ancestors. I *was* my ancestors. They were living in the world through me.

I owed them something more than grateful thoughts and deeds, more than hurried words between the deacon's prayer and the pastor's invitation to join church. I'd come to a new appreciation of the spiritual world, and the rituals of my past couldn't bear the strain.

"Tell me what to do," I begged them. "I want to go somewhere, to step apart and show you how much I love you."

They took me right there in the car. My hands were on the wheel, my eyes were on the road, but part of my consciousness had left the natural world. I poured myself into the vision, afraid of losing the tiniest detail.

When I got home after work that evening, I wrote to a friend. I told her everything: the beach on the ocean; seven white candles standing in the sand; an open Bible; and me in white, singing and standing in the water.

"Take this to your spiritual mother, and ask her what it means," I wrote.

My friend called me a couple of days later. "Mother wants you to call her immediately," she said. "You've got to go to Trinidad. You've got to be baptized."

Chapter Nineteen

The saints in Trinidad don't sing "Wade in the Water." The elders huddled around my spiritual mother, Pamela Taylor, when I raised the song as proof of my conversion. She explained its history and meaning: a melody created by African slaves, sung as a signal to gather for escape; lifted at baptisms as the candidates waited to enter the pool. Meanwhile, I stood off to the side, taking an unexpected opportunity to contemplate the new journey I was starting.

Mother had explained that my vision—a circle of candles buried in the sand, with an open Bible in the middle; me in white, standing in the ocean—had all the makings of a Spiritual Baptist ritual. When she finished, I only asked one question.

"What is Spiritual Baptist?"

It is a Trinidadian religion, she explained, and the ebb and flow of her voice invoked an island I had never seen. The faith is marked by signs and symbols. Its believers are called by dreams and visions.

The Scriptures warn that obedience is better than sacrifice. This time, I didn't hesitate or worry about abandoning my Christianity. Really, I wasn't leaving my faith behind; I was still a Baptist, but one of a different sort. Becoming a Spiritual Baptist hinted at a deeper, richer communion with the spirits and guides I longed to reach. I'd come out the water once and my life had changed. I could go back in and come out again if it meant experiencing new depths in God.

My assurance wavered, though, when our van dropped us off for the ritual. Five of us had come to Trinidad. Two of us were to go into the water, and we'd waited impatiently for this evening.

We'd envisioned ourselves standing at the mouth of a river where the sea mingled with the sweet, fresh water. We would be gathered under a canopy of coconut palms, raising our white skirts to keep them clean and dry. The waves would roll in softly and lap at our feet, as if Yemaya and Oshun themselves had come to welcome us.

Instead, we were let off in the city, not in the country. No trees grew on this scrap of land, just grass that was thigh high in places.

Tangled vines grew up the side of a metal gate that kept trespassers away from something. But the treasure worth protecting was nowhere in sight. It was long gone, maybe moved to a more desirable spot, or maybe it had simply fallen down and decayed.

An abandoned shed testified to the fact that, once, this place had been used. But that was years ago. Weather had cracked the wooden planks on the roof. Salt and humidity rusted the sheets of metal covering the old windows. Clearly, no one cared about this place. Even the locals glanced here and looked away, preferring more soothing scenery.

My friend, Shirley, shook her head no, when I invited her to walk around with me. I'd only met her when I arrived at the airport, but I'd already come to depend on her cheerfulness and serenity. This evening, though, disappointment was all she could manage. She propped her arm on the back of the seat in front of her, and rested her head in her hand.

I shrugged and put my camera around my neck. I'd come too far to let a little trash on the beach dampen my spirits. The light was fading fast, and I'd left my flash back in the United States. I wanted to take some pictures to help me remember this day.

But I felt as disappointed as my friend. I'd been so sure about my calling when I talked to Mother Taylor. Had my heart overcome my head? Had I been relying on my own, meager understanding instead of following a directive from the spirits?

Like Joshua and Hezekiah, I asked for a sign.

I wandered aimlessly to a bunch of straggly plants. Their brown stems contrasted nicely against the sand, and I hoped the composition would make a good picture. I walked around, then squatted to find the best angle. I'd focused my lens when I saw the stalks ended in little bolls filled with soft, fluffy fiber.

I frowned, not quite believing what I was seeing. I plucked a boll and shredded the strands between my fingers.

It was cotton, not the carefully cultivated plants I'd seen in Mississippi, but cotton nonetheless. The little bolls had held black Americans in authentic and virtual slavery for most of our history in the United States, as surely as if the blossoms were a ball and chain.

No one in my family had come from Trinidad. No island blood of any kind flowed through my veins. I'd traced us back to the mid-nineteenth century and never found a homeplace other than the plantation in Williamson County, Tennessee. Yet, here I was, an ocean away from home, and I stumbled upon a plant that symbolized my people's history of oppression.

This wasn't the reassurance I would have hoped for, but it was the reassurance I needed. I was in the right place, heading in the right direction. I plucked a few bolls for my altar at home, and tucked them in the pocket of my skirt.

I'd raised the camera to my face, when I heard Mother Taylor calling my name. It was time to come and change into my whites. The baptismal ceremony was about to begin.

The similarity to all I'd known ended with the clothes and the cotton growing from the sand. The elders blindfolded me and the ritual started.

I'd been called, for sure, to become another Baptist, a Spiritual Baptist. This was the religion of slaves, who combined their traditional beliefs with Christianity, the Jewish Kabala, even with the Hinduism that arrived with the islands's Indian immigrants. It was a middle ground, I figured, a compromise that my ancestors fashioned to ease me further down the road toward them. I could pray the Lord's Prayer and honor the saints, knowing I was also talking to the Orisha and my ancestors. The Spiritual Baptist religion wasn't part of my heritage. But it felt enough like the religion I knew to satisfy me for a minute, while the Spirits took me further down the road.

Music kept me in the black church. I didn't long for the hymns or the newer, upbeat gospel songs. I hungered for the meandering chants lifted from the congregation.

"Jesus, Jesus, Jesus . . . in my heart, I've got the love of Jesus in my heart."

The melody turned me inside out until I lost the consciousness of my self. I wasn't singing for or about Jesus. I wasn't even an individual, whose voice joined those of folks sitting beside me.

I was the song. I was the notes that flowed from major to minor, from joy to sadness. I was the emotion written between the lines of the lyrics. I was everyone now singing and everyone who had ever sung.

I'd transcended my personality to merge into a collective identity. I was standing on my feet, swaying from side to side, watching myself shrink and give way to something larger and stronger.

I was possessed.

Who could I tell? Who would understand this transformation? At best, possession meant dancing and shouting at the direction of the Holy Spirit. At worst, it meant fighting off Satan's attack. The saints around me would have urged me to plead the blood of Jesus, to chant his name until the enemy retreated. They wouldn't have understood the quiet conquest occurring in plain sight.

Yet this was not the way that the Orishas arrived. They dismissed the individual's personality until they were ready to leave.

I was partly conscious. I could remember and recite everything that happened while I stood singing. I was standing on the sidelines of myself, like a spectator observing the scene from the balcony instead of the first floor.

The spirits had me. They'd arrived in songs that spoke to the core of my experience.

Unity and Yoruba shaped my cosmology and theology. But the more involved I became with the Orishas, the more I missed the old songs. I hadn't felt Yemaya, might never be a vessel of hers. But I'd sat just a pew away from Grandma Moore almost every Sunday of my childhood.

And she loved Jesus, in her heart.

"... *I want to be like Jesus, I want to be like Jesus in my heart* ..."

When the song ended and we all sat down, I lingered in my special psychic space.

I was a pilgrim, just like my great-grandmother had been. She'd been pressing onward to heaven, but I just wanted somewhere to belong.

The church lauded God the Father and Jesus the Son, but offered no words for the people whose struggles had ensured my success. I couldn't stay there. I was looking for a home.

I prepared my altar the way the priestess had told me. Nine glasses of water reflected the sturdy flame from the white candle. I made a special trip to the Catholic store to buy a seven-day candle in a glass container. The wax didn't smoke or burn soot when I lit the wick, and I felt better about letting it burn the entire week.

I brought a special table, no makeshift foundation this time. Besides, I needed a larger surface to hold everything I had. I brought a new package of Lucky Strikes and tiny bottle of scotch on my last plane trip. These were Daddy's favorites; I felt anger and regret every time I looked at them. But we couldn't judge our ancestors. We were to accept them as they were. He loved liquor and tobacco. I loved him.

It was time to pray.

I read this prayer slowly. The unfamiliar sounds of Yoruba hindered me. I hoped my crude pronunciation wouldn't turn a blessing into a curse. But this was the best I could do.

My ancestors would forgive me, if they could understand me.

The prayer ended the ritual, but I couldn't leave. Things felt unsettled, as if the ancestors were expecting more. I reached for the first song that came to mind, skipping past the verses to the chorus, reminding myself that, whatever religion I practiced, God knew my heart.

PART FOUR

Chapter Twenty

In the beginning I saw my research as a straight line, carrying me back to my family's origins in Africa. I wanted to put my finger on the exact place where slave catchers took the ancestor whose ordeal begat a family in Tennessee. That was the truth of Sankofa, I thought. You retrieve the lost treasure merely by turning around and retracing your steps.

The years clarified my vision and deepened my understanding. Sankofa is a circuitous journey, subject to interruptions, distractions, and surprises. No wonder the Akan rendered the proverb as a pair of connected curves that mirror each other. The journey back is full of reflections. The pauses come when you stop to linger over your actions, to consider the road you chose to take you away. Instead, it brought you back to the starting point. What goes around comes around, but no one returns unchanged. In finding what you'd lost, you confront the person you were, from the vantage point of who you have become.

As my research continued, I grew closer to the dead than the living. I didn't know their idiosyncrasies or all the nuances of their personalities that gave them life. Still, I knew their names. Sometimes I knew when they were born. Most times I knew when they'd died. The facts accumulated until I could speak authoritatively and comfortably about people long lost to me. I had a relationship with them simply by virtue of my tenacity and patience. I could link my ancestors, one by one, and construct a virtual family, if not a real one. I knew who should follow whom, whose descendants branched off and where.

That was why I was so satisfied with my work when I reviewed the notes in my red spiral book. I turned the pages carefully. They were soft and worn from too much handling. This drugstore binder was not meant to become the archive of my family line.

When I looked at the names, I checked to make sure sweat hadn't smeared the ink. I'd jotted down a lot of this information early in my research. Some of those notes were crossed out, then rewritten when the first impression turned out to be the correct one. Over the years I'd gone back, I'd learned something with each rereading.

At first I hadn't even known whether Sofia Ann Brown was related to me. Her name had caught my eye because Browns and Scruggses had intermarried. She'd been born a Scruggs; Dick was her father and a woman named Lucy Barnes was her mother. That meant Dick had had two wives, or maybe more.

Usually I stopped there. But this time I checked to see who'd provided the information for the death certificate. The informant sometimes turned out to be a spouse or close relative. When I got to the end of the entry, I stopped. The informant's name was Washington Brown.

I had copied the information down myself, but I'd overlooked the significance of that name for years. Suddenly the

snide remarks and knowing chuckles that had mystified my father and his siblings made perfect sense.

I called Cousin Bertha just to make sure. She would know
better than I. I kept the niceties short, offering just the flimsiest
of greetings before I got to my point.

"Dock Brown, Aunt Ann's husband. Was he my granddaddy's daddy?"

Her laughter answered my question.

"Were there other children?"

She ticked them off. "Richard, Florence, and Washington
Brown. And those are the ones that we knew about."

There wasn't much left for me to say. "Well, you take care.
Thanks for talking to me."

"All right."

I was shaking my head when I hung up the telephone. The
skeleton in my family's closet didn't belong to a white man but
a black one. I didn't doubt that the white Scruggses had enslaved their black family members. But that was someone else's
family, not mine.

What kind of family tree would I construct now? The
branches didn't extend straight and strong. They were gnarled
and tangled, like a thorny, overgrown hedge.

Mama laughed too when I called to tell her what I'd
learned. "I told you to leave that mess alone. . . ." she said.

No, she hadn't known. She'd just figured something had
been buried and she didn't see any reason to dig up old bones.
Let them rest in peace.

How old would my grandfather have been then, in his late
seventies or early eighties? He'd been dead at least fifty years
when I stumbled upon the facts of his birth. Still, Cousin Bertha
couldn't or wouldn't answer my question directly. Nor had she

explained years before, when she gave me my ancestors' names.

The secret cut deeply and so efficiently, you wouldn't feel the pain until you saw the blood. Time hadn't dulled its treacherous edge and it was still best handled with care.

I had been born almost thirty years after my grandfather's death. I hadn't even known about his parents. Still I was shocked.

My grandfather's father had been his uncle. His maternal aunt was, for all practical purposes, his stepmother. And the children who were his first cousins on his mother's side were his siblings on his father's side.

Julia, my great-grandmother, had her first child at thirteen. She was probably nursing her twins when she was shot. She was an experienced mother at seventeen, with four children by three different men.

This sounded like the story of a dysfunctional family, headed for welfare and drugs. Yet I graduated college and made my family proud.

What had changed in a hundred years?

I prayed for my period. Every day for two weeks, the words fell from my mouth. Sometimes I pushed them aside, so I could answer my professors or talk with the girls studying in the dormitory lounge. But those were temporary distractions. Most of the time I pleaded for blood that failed to appear.

"Do you want an abortion?" The counselor at the makeshift clinic knew the answer before I nodded my head. She explained the procedure, pausing at times to see if I really understood. I'd have to go to New York or Kansas City; in 1971, they were the closest places to obtain a legal abortion.

"New York," I decided. "I have friends there." They knew the abortion clinic. They'd been there.

The operation cost two hundred dollars, not including the air or train fare. I pulled the money together somehow, some way made it there and back to Chicago.

When my parents came to town and demanded a meeting, I didn't flinch when my mother pulled out the brochures I'd hidden. I didn't stutter. I didn't reach for an explanation. I'd been through enough, lying on a table with my legs in stirrups, clenching my fists to keep from moaning in pain. My parents might punish me for lying, make me come so they could watch over me. But I could handle them now.

I wasn't pregnant anymore. That was all that mattered.

"Why didn't you tell us?" Mama didn't accuse me. She was, I think, sincerely hurt that I'd taken my life into my own hands, without even a thought of involving her.

"You'd have thrown it up in my face." Daddy smiled at the truth of that one.

"Who paid for it?"

The boy had given some of the money. The rest I'd gotten myself. Mama looked at me, finally understanding the distance I'd traveled since I'd left home nine months earlier. I was just sixteen when I left for school. She'd worried whether I'd survive the year, or come home high and addicted. I had worried that my grades wouldn't cut it, that I'd come home in academic disgrace.

Neither one of us had counted on the evolutions that occurred: my long hair ending up on the floor of a barber shop; my speech coarsening; my preference for staying with my friends in Chicago instead of visiting family in Nashville. I was developing a mind of my own.

"I didn't want to get married," I answered firmly.

I didn't want to be eighteen with a child and a too-young husband. I refused to sacrifice my ambitions because I'd gotten off the pill for a month and believed my boyfriend really could pull out in time. I'd made a huge mistake. I'd been stupid, but I wasn't a fool.

"You could have come home. . . ."

I could have stepped into prison and handed the key to the warden. I could have confronted my father's disappointment over the opportunity I'd squandered.

No; I regretted the pregnancy, but not the abortion. Definitely not the abortion.

My parents looked at me, still awed that I'd gotten myself in—and out—of this predicament. My mother knew that, if I'd asked, she'd probably have arranged an abortion herself. But the procedure would have been performed on a dirty table in a back room, without anesthesia, nurses, or empathy.

"Just promise us you won't see the boy anymore," Daddy said.

We knew I was lying when I agreed. So shortly afterwards I ended up in Nashville for the summer, where they could watch me walk away from them, into my own life.

My father seemed to accept my transformation easier than my mother had.

"You know, once you start having sex, you don't stop."

We were in the den. He was stretched out on the sofa, comfortable in spite of the vinyl cushions. I'd brought him a glass of scotch and water. His cigarettes lay next to his drink.

"Yeah, I know." I shifted, but didn't leave. I respected him too much to walk away when he so obviously wanted to talk.

"I want you to use protection next time. . . ."

I'd skipped the pills for a month because I'd been too broke to buy them.

He looked at me again, measuring who I'd become. I was old enough to have sex, but immature enough to get pregnant—and capable enough to come to my own solution.

"You know, your aunt thought you were on drugs. . . ."

"Drugs?!"

"She saw that powdered milk you threw away. . . ."

We both howled. My aunt was such a stickler for order, she even had a special routine for washing dishes. A dishpan full of soapy water sat in one sink. The other sink held the rinse water. You washed the dishes in the dishpan, then stacked them in the rinse water. When you finished, you put all the dishes into the drain rack, and let the air dry them.

I transgressed constantly, breaking rules I didn't know existed. When I poured out too much non-fat dry milk for some hot chocolate, I looked around to see if she was in the kitchen. Then I swept the milk into the dustpan and threw it in the bathroom wastebasket.

She had seen the powder and decided it was heroin or cocaine.

"Why didn't you flush it down the toilet?" Daddy asked.

"Oh, the water would have turned white and foamy. Then what could I say?"

Daddy broke out laughing again. "I told your Mama you weren't on drugs. Nobody throws dope away."

"Yeah, that would be stupid." As stupid as having sex without using contraceptives.

He sipped his drink. The talk moved on to other topics. I didn't suspect how he'd really felt until years later, right before he died. He fretted about the grandchildren he might never see, and whether another generation would carry on our name.

*   *   *

What would my family have gained if my grandfather had been a legitimate Brown? What could he have claimed if he'd stood with Richard, Washington, and Florence, instead of Jerry, Elnora, and Dora?

The basic facts of his life would not have changed. His parents' affair was no cross-county dalliance, no city-slicker–country-girl fling. Washington Brown and Julia Scruggs lived in and around the same crossroads. The same first names ran through both families. Hadn't Washington's brother, William, married Emma, a Scruggs sister herself? Hadn't William heard his own name whenever he called for his nephew? Intermarriage and cross-relationships insured that the cousins—Emma's nine, Ann's three, and at least one of Julia's—were virtual siblings.

Still, my grandfather faced whispers and winks. The gossip attached to his name was passed down to his children and beyond. What if William had stood with his cousins and siblings, in the midst of the Browns, instead of off to one side?

The Browns were a mixed family. The father, Washington, had been a slave who had belonged to a white man named Ben Brown. The mother, Catherine "Katie" Poynor, had been a slave too. When the master Robert died, Catherine, her siblings, and her family were allotted to his children. The division was a formality, though, because the entire family stayed together. White and black, they were all the master's descendants.

The black Poynors weren't distinguished by their ancestry but by their father's skill. Dick Poynor was a master chair maker.

He might have learned from his father, whose estate inventory included tools for making chairs. Or he might have learned from another slave; such craftsmen were valued by plantation owners.

Still, Robert, the master, owned the tools and the man who used them. Eventually, though, Dick profited from his skill. He made chairs by the hundreds, enough to establish a factory, enough to buy his freedom and that of his first wife. When Union soldiers brought an emancipation that left so many slaves to their own devices, Dick's chairs supported his family. After he died, they survived to carry on his name and reputation.

"Come here." The librarian at the Williamson County archives led me down the aisle to artifacts displayed on a shelf above the rows of file cabinets. She stopped below a rocker and pointed to it proudly.

Dick Poynor had been a man of standards. He only used green maple for the chair frames, and dried hickory for the rungs. He marked his work with a small design recognizable to the cognoscenti, but subtle enough for an imitator to ignore.

"It's beautiful," I said, marveling over the longevity of this piece of furniture. Dick had died well before the turn of the twentieth century. The chair was a good one hundred and fifty years old. Yet the wood remained sturdy, impervious to time and weather. This chair was a heritage worth claiming.

"How are you related to Dick Poynor?"

I turned to the librarian and smiled. "My grandfather was his . . ." I paused to count the generations, ". . . his great-grandson."

"What was your grandfather's name?"

"William Scruggs," I said, putting him with his family, where he belonged. "William Scruggs."

Epilogue I

Once again I was seated at a table, pulling out pens and paper. Once again I was talking about family. But this one wasn't mine, or at least I didn't think it was. The trio in front of me were siblings: Jack, Vernice, and Barbara Ragin. They were Scruggses, just like me. But they were the true descendants of Ned Scruggs.

Their complexion and features testified to their heritage. Their skin was light, almost identical to Cousin Bertha's in its paleness. But they had blue eyes, bright and clear enough to match the sky on a brilliant summer morning. Both my skin and eyes are deep brown, and far darker than theirs. Even the lightest person in my family, my brother, would not have come close to their complexion.

Once I would have considered the differences and seen the distance between us. But more than twenty years of digging through records, writing and rewriting information, and reading and rereading notes had brought me a new awareness of the meaning of a family. Blood mattered. But connections and shared experience counted as much—or sometimes even more.

We had much in common, the Ragins and I. We were

Southerners come North. And although they were older than I, we'd gone through the same acclimation process. We shivered in Cleveland's winters, learning how to walk on ice and snow. We became accustomed to summers when breezes, not air conditioning, cooled our homes.

We'd set aside our Southern accents, picking them up only when we returned home.

This was our first meeting, true, but we'd talked a couple times. In fact, they knew me better than I knew them. My shift from academia to journalism had taken me out of the South and brought me to the Midwest. I'd finally landed in Cleveland, where I became a columnist. With three articles a week, I couldn't hide from the readers. My writing revealed my sarcastic sense of humor, and my passion for history and heritage.

For black history month, I'd written about my great-great-grandfather's life as a slave in Williamson County. I got three hundred calls about the piece; probably a hundred from all the Scruggses between Cleveland, Akron, and Columbus.

But one call got my attention. A young woman said her family was from middle Tennessee too. Her name was Jackie Ragin. But her grandmother had been a Scruggs.

Her grandmother said they were related to a white man named Ned. But Jackie seemed a little skeptical about the information; she said her grandmother had a speech impediment.

"No she didn't," I answered. "That was his name."

"You know him?"

"Sure," I answered. "That's a well-known story down there. I know who you are. You're related to Gus and Cannon and Pete. You're related to a woman named 'Ariah, or Mariah, I'm not sure which."

Jackie listened as I rattled off all I'd learned about Scruggses, white and black. I told her about old man Ed Scruggs's death, the way the slaves had been inventoried and divided.

When I finished, she asked about Ned. "Are you related to him?"

"Nope."

"Are you sure?"

I spoke firmly. "I'm sure. We should have been Browns."

Now, five years after that conversation, I was sitting with Jackie's father and her aunts. Twenty years had passed since my father's death inspired my search to understand what it meant to be a Scruggs. I'd started with Ned back then, and I was ending with him now.

The circle was almost closed.

Jack pulled out a slip of yellow paper and carefully unfolded it. His family lineage was listed on a note much smaller than the legal pads I used. He'd written two names on one line: Ned Scruggs and Mariah Elison. I nodded as I copied his notes. I'd seen Mariah in the census records, with two, then three sons and a daughter. But she'd been listed as a Scruggs. "Her last name was Elison?" I asked.

"I talked to four people and they told me her name was Elison," he said. "Everybody knew her. They called her 'Grandma Ri.' "

The next line contained the names of three sons: Cannon, Gus, and Pete. Underneath each man's name, Jack had written a list of their descendants.

"We came from him," Jack said, as he pointed to Burt Scruggs, one of Cannon's four children.

"Was his name Burton?" I wondered. I'd found a Burton Scruggs on the old 1847 inventory and I thought the younger man had been named for the older one.

"No, Burt," Jack corrected me. "His name was Burt."

Burt had married Barbara Reid. Their daughter, Louise, was

the grandmother with the alleged speech impediment.

"What speech impediment?" Barbara Ragin said. "Mama didn't have a speech impediment."

"Look, I'm just a reporter," I joked, holding up my hands in playful surrender. "I'm just telling you the conversation the way I remember it."

We looked at the other names. Gus Scruggs had fathered seven children; Pete had four. Names I'd seen for years suddenly made sense: Jack and Clyde were Pete's sons; Gus senior was their uncle; and Columbus, Andrew, and Gus junior were his children.

I pointed to Gus senior. "I think he was my great-uncle's father," I said.

Barbara looked puzzled. "Then how come you aren't part of this?"

"Because my great-uncle and my grandfather had different fathers. They were half brothers."

The Ragins rolled their eyes and I shook my head. They'd run into the same silence that had hindered me. They knew how hard it was to chip a hole in the walls that had kept us from our heritage. As we swapped stories of who was truly a Scruggs—and who wasn't—I realized that this was all of a piece. The dormant stories and the whispered comments were as legitimate as facts and dates. I'd wanted to correct the record; after all, I was a scholar and a journalist. But the omissions and mistakes were the record, and they belonged there. Without them, our heritage would become boring recitations of marriages and divorces, of births and deaths.

Ours is the story of our relationship to our loved ones, no matter how many—or how few—facts we actually know. That relationship makes us hunch over fading documents and rub our strained eyes as we try to decipher a letter or a name. It's the reason we hover over reticent relatives until they acquiesce and answer our questions. It fuels our frustration over our inability to tie up loose ends.

In reality, there are no loose ends. The family lines fray, but the circle remains unbroken.

By now the Ragin siblings had come down to their generation. They were arguing over names and nicknames, parents and lineage. How many of these conversations had I heard over my mother's kitchen table? How many of these arguments had I had with my sister?

I bit my lip to keep from laughing out loud. This is life. This is the way the past survives and tints the present. This is the way the ancestors stand on the margins and look over us. I listened to Barbara arguing with Jack, and I marveled at the sweet complexity of the cosmos.

Back in the 1800s, when slavery was making its death rattle, Ned Scruggs and Mariah Elison had had three children. Maybe he loved her, like the white insurance agent claimed. Or maybe Ned Scruggs had caught a black woman in the bushes of Scruggs Bottom and raped her, like the old women had told Jack.

But the story of Ned and Mariah survived: in a legend still told; in the documents that survived Ned's death; and in the persons of Gus, Cannon, and Pete, their sons.

Back around the turn of the twentieth century, a young girl had two sons by different men. One son was the son of the elder Gus Scruggs. Her sister's husband fathered the second son—my grandfather.

Through blood and proximity, the lines merged: Scruggses with Scruggses and Browns and others. Then life did its job and death helped. Guardians died, and children were sent to live with others. The families separated and almost dissolved.

Almost.

A century later, I'm sitting with people I've just met, talking about people that I'd never met. Yet we toss names back and forth as if we were raised up together.

We had come back together that afternoon in Barbara's kitchen. The tie binding us had not broken.

Jack stopped talking with his sister and turned to me. He looked at the notes I'd taken. "Well, do you think we're related?" he asked.

I hesitated, weighing facts against truth until I knew how to answer. "I don't know," I admitted. "But you know what? It doesn't matter.

"It really doesn't matter at all."

Epilogue II

I'd lived in Nashville long enough to know the capricious nature of the city's spring. Saturday had been sunny, and so hot I had to beg my teenaged nieces for clothes. Sunday I shivered in my thin Easter dress and open-toed shoes. Still, the weather was a respite. Back home in Cleveland, so-called spring brought clouds and gloom. In Nashville, at least the sun was playing hide and seek with the rain clouds.

I was in the van with my brother and his children. We were on our way to the national cemetery. The kids sat in the back seats, shouting and laughing, doing all the things kids do to make a long trip shorter. We really weren't going far, though, just a half-hour ride from my mother's house. The kids looked at it as an excursion.

But we adults sat somberly in the front seat. This wasn't a pleasure trip. We were going to see our father.

In its way, the weather fit our mood. We weren't sad, but we weren't happy. As we drove closer to the cemetery, the pauses between our conversations lengthened until we'd stopped talking altogether. The kids' chatter grew noisier and noisier. But I resisted the urge to turn around and make them hush. Why should I put an end to their good time?

Their father sat upfront, right next to me.

My daddy was in the ground.

My mother had refused to come. She said she didn't like graveyards. "I'm afraid I'll walk over a grave and fall in," she said. She spent Easter at the latest church of her choice—Mama changed denominations every couple of years or so. This time she tried to entice me to go with her. "The kids are singing and they need a good musician," she said.

"They have a good musician," I answered from the bed.

The entire choir had stopped by the house on Saturday for an impromptu rehearsal. I taught the song to them and their pianist because I absolutely would not be sitting in her church for four hours. I had a schedule to keep.

I left for my church, way across town, and arrived in time for the sermon, offering, and benediction. I was back home by 11 A.M.—when the congregants would have been straggling in at Mama's church. I wanted to be at the cemetery before noon.

But my brother had a schedule of his own. He rolled down our concrete driveway around 1 P.M. We didn't get there until 1:30.

My sister had promised she'd come down from Chattanooga, and then begged off at the last minute. Her decision ended hopes I'd had for a family reunion of sorts. Easter Sunday, March 29, 1997, was the anniversary of my father's birth. I'd wanted all of us to observe the day at his grave. Instead I settled for the people I got: my brother, three of his children, and me.

Who was I anyway? For years I'd kept my family at a physical distance. Now I was trying to round them up. We just weren't the type of people that put everything aside to gather for important occasions. There was always an empty seat at our table. My brother's excuse was his karate business; lessons and tournaments took up his time. My sister was dedicated to her teacher's union.

And I was just plain apprehensive and defensive about staying home for too long. Geography allowed me to keep my folks at arm's length, communicating with them on my own terms and at my convenience.

Still, I loved and missed them. I loved my father and missed him, too. I hadn't realized how I still grieved for him until Max junior and I stood staring at the small white headstone.

My mother had given us convoluted directions to Daddy's grave. "The gravestone number either has two threes and a four; or two fours and a three," she said.

Max didn't even listen. He didn't stop to check the index when we got to the cemetery, either. The endless rows of identical markers didn't confuse him at all. He drove straight to Daddy's grave, number four-thirty-four. "It's in line with that little tree," he said, pointing to a landmark way across the road.

The tree was young and small, and its buds shimmered in the heavy March mist. But it had already spread branches. In a few years this sapling would be large and strong. How would we locate Daddy's grave then?

We stood there silently, united by our individual thoughts. My memories rewound from my father's deathbed in intensive care, through my teenaged years, back to my childhood. I'd put my father atop a pedestal that lifted him so high, I decided he was the tallest man in the world. He laughed when I told him so; he wasn't even six feet. Shortly afterwards, he brought home a friend whose bright red hair seemed to brush the ceiling. But that didn't change my mind. I decided this man was really tall, if he was taller than the tallest man in the world.

My memories stopped, and then fast-forwarded to my father lying in the hospital, dependent on tubes and machinery. He'd shrunk and his withered skin and muscles were dying cell by cell. He died in 1980.

I'd come to his grave in 1997. Nothing but dust lay in his casket now.

Our love kept Daddy alive.

My brother stood the way my father would have. His feet were planted on the ground, and his legs spread slightly to support himself. His arms were crossed over his torso, and he looked as strong as he imagined himself to be.

"What are you thinking?" I asked.

He didn't turn to face me when he answered. "It's a hell of a thing to see your name on a tombstone."

We'd been lucky, my siblings and I. We didn't see close relatives die until we were in our twenties. Our great-grandmother had died in 1978; the next year her oldest son passed away.

And the next year we faced our father's casket. We could no longer deceive ourselves into thinking that youth would stretch into eternal life. We would die, old or young, but we would die. One day our existence would be etched into a piece of stone.

Seventeen years had not softened the words carved so cleanly and precisely. "Max Walter Scruggs, Sr. March 30 1929–Nov. 13 1980."

I laughed at myself. "So his birthday really is on Monday, huh?"

Max raised his eyes from the grave and glanced at the tombstone, with its implications for his life.

"Really, it was March 30, 1930," he said. "Daddy told me

the doctor was drunk and messed up his birth certificate. You know, Daddy wasn't born in a hospital."

I grunted, thinking not about my father, but his mother, her legs up, exposed and in pain, trusting health and her baby's life to a doctor too drunk to remember the correct date. This humiliation was a truth of my father's birth, not the date, place, or the time.

How could I explain such debasement and embarrassment to the kids running on the grass?

My mother brought them so many Christmas gifts that one year their parents held her to a quota of two presents per child. These were youngsters who could say "McDonald's" and "Burger King" as soon as they could pronounce their own names. What would they know about standing in a relief line for food, or sharing a sweet roll four ways—and being happy to do it?

These children led comfortable, sheltered lives. They couldn't relate to the poverty my father had experienced. And neither could we.

He wouldn't have wanted it any other way. He measured his success by our comfort and accomplishments. We would take all he'd given us, add to it, and pass it down to another set of descendants. We would break the cycle the family had endured since slavery.

But I don't think he'd counted on the price of such upward mobility. The higher we climbed, the farther we moved from our roots. Our changing lives destroyed the context for the few stories that we'd gotten of his family. The tales stood by themselves, without a connection to our routine or our expectations for our future.

Out of the corner of my eye, I saw my youngest nephew Bakari running toward a newly dug grave.

"Hey, stop that!" I shouted at him just before he stepped on the fresh, clean hay. He skidded like the characters he'd seen on cartoons. His grin showed the gap where his baby teeth used to be. I wanted to laugh at his air-conditioned mouth. Instead I raised my eyebrows and narrowed my eyes. My mind-your-elders look didn't accomplish a darned thing.

"Why?" he wanted to know. "They're already dead."

But not gone. Somebody loved whoever lay in that plot. We had to acknowledge their love and grief, as well as the dead person's life. I didn't lecture Bakari; I softened my voice.

"You just don't play on graves. It's a matter of respect."

My brother waved his arms and herded us all back to the van. We'd come to mourn. The kids had come to play. Now there was nothing left to do, I figured, but head back home.

Instead Max cruised the road, going deeper and deeper into the cemetery. The headstones became smaller and rounder, worn down by decades of Nashville's rainy springs and icy winters.

"Look . . ." Max pointed with one hand, while steering with the other. He slowed down to a few miles an hour so the kids could read the names on the tombstones.

"Look at the dates . . ."

The kids exclaimed over the numbers: 1914, 1918, years before the birth of their great-grandmothers, the oldest people they knew.

"This is the section for World War One veterans," he told me. I was impressed. Obviously Max had been out here before. He just hadn't told any of us.

He turned and took us to another section. These tombstones had sunk in the ground as if tired of standing at attention. They hunched over like old men, too fragile to bear the weight of their uniforms. The initials CSA came after several names; these were the Confederate veterans.

The kids subtracted the numbers on the headstones, turning the years of a life into an arithmetic problem. The answers surprised them; some of these men had not lived to see twenty.

My niece and nephews were confronting history and shaping it to their own understanding. They would take what they needed from dates, events, and situations, and let time absorb the rest.

Maybe this process was the American version of Mbiti's Zamani.

I leaned back in my seat. We'd left the cemetery, trading its rolling hillocks and serenity for the noisy traffic of the broad highway. Max turned up the radio, and the kids teased and fought with each other in the back of the van.

The moments at Daddy's grave contained all I'd discovered about my family and our history. My brother and I had reflected on people we'd loved, the people we were, and the legacy we'd leave. I wanted to pass everything down to the kids behind me. I yearned for them to feel the same love I'd felt for Daddy.

But I could only share my experiences, and hope they'd understand it. My father was little more than a name to them, a photograph in a frame. They'd never touched his cheek or called him Granddaddy. He'd never lifted them high over his head the way he'd done with us.

My niece's and nephews' affection for him was filtered through the love they felt for their father—his son.

My father was blending into the shadows of time. I could hinder the process with my research and my stories, but I could not stop it.

One day I will die. My brother will die. His children will

talk of my father, if at all, in relation to us. But we will be mentioned less and less as the family stretches into the future.

One day, Max Walter Scruggs's name will finally disappear from the lips of his descendants.

That will be the day he finds his final rest in eternity.